AND THEN THERE WAS:

The U.S. president who declared, "If Lincoln were alive today, he would be rolling over in his grave."

The diner owner who collected spare change from his customers to help out Donald Trump.

The champion athlete whose career was wrecked when teammates cut off his long hair.

The International Lint Museum in Rutland, Vermont.

The propaganda kits to be dropped into North Vietnam—each containing a diamond pin and a pen-and-pencil set.

The Mafia hit man who forgot to load his gun; slipped and hit his head while trying to choke someone in a shower; tripped and fell on his own knife; and drove off a cliff while trying to force someone from the road.

YES, IT'S A MAD, MAD WORLD—AND NOW YOU CAN MEET ALL THE PEOPLE WHO MAKE IT THAT WAY!

FOLLIES, FOIBLES, AND FOOLISH DEEDS

A Compendium of Human Misadventure

by

Robert Cooper

A SIGNET BOOK

SIGNET
Published by the Penguin Group
Penguin Books USA Inc., 375 Hudson Street,
New York, New York 10014, U.S.A.
Penguin Books Ltd, 27 Wrights Lane,
London W8 5TZ, England
Penguin Books Australia Ltd, Ringwood,
Victoria, Australia
Penguin Books Canada Ltd, 10 Alcorn Avenue,
Toronto, Ontario, Canada M4V 3B2
Penguin Books (N.Z.) Ltd, 182–190 Wairau Road,
Auckland 10, New Zealand

Penguin Books Ltd, Registered Offices:
Harmondsworth, Middlesex, England

First published by Signet, an imprint of New American Library,
a division of Penguin Books USA Inc.

First Printing, August, 1993
10 9 8 7 6 5 4 3 2 1

This book is dedicated
to those who have made it possible.

Whether the human race gains in
wisdom as time goes by is uncertain;
the one thing we can be sure of is
that its absurdities take changing forms.

—*Frederick Lewis Allen*

CONTENTS

INTRODUCTION

Folly Lives

Several years ago in Detroit a man tried to rob a bank—from a remote drive-in window.

In Los Angeles a woman married a fifty-pound rock.

In Arizona a woman whose house had been struck by lightning sued God for negligence.

Is there any end to human folly? Apparently not—as this book attests. The follies gathered here speak loudly—even shout—that fools have always been with us, are with us now, and will be with us to the end. See for yourself by reading your daily newspaper or weekly newsmagazine. Better yet, directly observe other members of your species. From arts to business to government to science, from the U.S. to France to Pakistan to Japan, fools are everywhere—there is no escape. In fact, when it comes right down to it we might have to paraphrase cartoon character Pogo and say, "We have met the fool—and he is us."

CRIME

Fool For a Lawyer

Marshall Cummings, on trial in Tulsa, Oklahoma, decided to serve as his own lawyer. He was accused of snatching a woman's purse. All went well until he questioned the woman whose purse he was accused of snagging. He asked her, "Did you get a good look at my face when I took your purse?"

Cummings was sentenced to ten years in the Oklahoma State Penitentiary.

Beautiful Corterra

Many residents of Hong Kong—especially the well-off—are desperately arranging to emigrate before China takes over the colony in 1997. The Federal Republic of Corterra sounded like an ideal place to live. It was advertised as a tiny Pacific island between Tahiti and Hawaii, with a population of 80,000, a democratic government, a British-style legal system and no income tax. Best of all, a Corterra passport could be had in Hong Kong for only $16,000. A number of local businessmen quickly paid the application fee of $5,000. There was only one problem: Corterra does not exist.

Safe Drive

One night a pair of thieves in Canoga Park, California, stole a six thousand pound safe from the front of a lock and safe shop. They were extremely stealthy. They tied a nylon strap around the safe, then dragged it away with a car. Said one witness: "It looked like they were towing a Roman candle." Said another: "I heard a big thundering noise. When I looked out my window, I saw the car coming down the street with sparks flying all over the place. The ground was shaking." After quickly apprehending thieves, the police let them in on a little secret: the safe was empty.

Wrong Peel

On January 20, 1843, near Charing Cross, London, a thirty-year-old wood turner named Daniel McNaughton walked up and shot Edward Drummond from behind at point blank range. Mistake number one: it was broad daylight on a busy thoroughfare. Mistake number two: he slowly and calmly placed the first pistol in his pocket and drew a second. This casual approach allowed a police officer to grab his arm and throw him to the ground. Mistake number three: the man he had shot was not Prime Minister Robert Peel, his intended victim, but Peel's private secretary.

Relaxed Burglars

A forty-three-year-old man burgled a house in Burbank, California, ransacking the place before he happened on a nice bottle of wine. Apparently it was good wine, because he drank the whole bottle, and was passed out on the sofa when the homeowner returned some time later. He was so deep in slumber that the police had a hard time waking him up.

Another would-be burglar, this one twenty-one, passed out while burglarizing the residence of an elderly couple in Van Nuys, California. The wife stepped on him while climbing out of bed. This swift fellow had downed twenty beers before breaking into the house.

"A criminal is a person with predatory instincts who has not sufficient capital to form a corporation."
—*Howard Scott*

Self-destruct

In the fall of 1990, police found the charred body of a woman in the desert outside San Bernadino,

California. She had been so badly burned that there was no way of identifying her. Shortly afterward, they got lucky: a man whose wife was missing contacted them, and conveniently provided them with his wife's dental X-rays. From these they made a positive identification, and shortly thereafter arrested the helpful fellow for murdering his wife.

Long Trip

After the United States won independence from England, the latter had to find a new dumping ground for criminals. They chose Australia. Convicts there were treated brutally. So much so, that they frequently tried to escape. Not brilliant in geography, some set out to walk back to England; others, better educated, realized that Australia is an island—they stole canoes and tried to row back.

Needs His Beer

In Maywood, California, a young motorist really needed his beer. When advised at 5:40 a.m. that stores were not allowed to sell beer between 2 and 6 a.m., Jehzeel Narchena was somewhat put out. He cut a few "donuts" around the Arco Market/Gas Station, then smashed into a fuel pump, causing an explosion that sent flames shooting 150 feet into the air. The $500,000 in damage included his own car, which was burned beyond recognition.

Superstitious Burglar

In Taipei, Taiwan, a taxi driver burglarized a gas station. Before leaving, he performed a traditional Taiwanese ritual to ward off any bad luck. The ritual? He squatted down and defecated in an office on the second floor. The police caught him with his pants down.

Fill Her Up

In 1985, a TWA airliner was hijacked in the Near East with 153 passengers on board. The flight kept getting shunted from Beirut to Algiers and back again. On one landing in Beirut, the hijackers demanded fuel, threatening to kill one passenger every five minutes until they got it. But the ground crew was adamant: *no fuel without payment.* However, they *were* generous enough to accept a flight attendant's Shell credit card instead of cash.

Fun for the Whole Family

At one time, English landowners could legally set mechanical traps for poachers and other trespassers. An 1861 law prohibited such devices— but it was still legal to catch trespassers in pits. One Lord Spencer dug a pit twelve feet deep and eight feet across in the middle of a path through his woods, covered the pit with quick-opening doors, and concealed the doors with grass and dirt. Of course this unusual project, for which he used local labor, was instantly known to every poacher in the area, and they all naturally avoided it. But the trap did manage to catch foxes, rabbits, pheasants, wild boars, a pair of strolling lovers and—best of all—a complete family of four who had gone into the woods for a picnic.

". . . in Chicago—it is unwise to take your eyes off any asset smaller than a locomotive."
— Keith Wheeler

Pub(l)ic Exposure

Iranian student Mehrdad Dashti took hostages in Berkeley, California in 1990 because he had many grievances—one of them with San Francisco police over charges that he had stolen checks. This explains one of his demands during the tense standoff: he wanted San Francisco Police Chief Frank Jordan to pull down his pants on television.

Serious Drawing

Until 1790, criminals in England were burned alive for serious offenses. They were "drawn" to the gallows and then roasted. Being "drawn" originally meant being tied to a horse's tail and dragged, but this was eventually changed, so that prisoners could be transported to the stake on sledges. According to the great English jurist Blackstone, the change showed "the humanity of the English nation."

Ducking Stool

As recently as the 1960s, "ducking" was still the legal punishment in New Jersey and Pennsylvania for men who swore and women who talked too much. What is "ducking"? You put a chair on the end of a seesaw, tie a person in the chair, and then "duck" the chair in a stream.

Horrible Language

In 1757, a Frenchman named Damiens, tried to assassinate King Louis XV. For this noble effort, the good fellow was:

1. drawn on a hurdle to the scaffold,
2. torn with red-hot pincers,
3. broken on the wheel (but not killed),
4. had his fingers and toes crushed,
5. had four horses tied to his arms and feet and driven in opposite directions, while
6. the executioner dropped sealing wax on his body.

During this process, the victim was shouting at the top of his lungs. A nearby spectator, hard of hearing, asked a friend what the man was saying. "I can't repeat it," the friend replied, "he's using horrible language."

Magical Powers

A fortune teller in Huntington Beach, California, was charged with fraud for bilking customers out of half a million dollars. She spun promises of magic powers conferred only on believers who turned over their worldly goods to her "meditation groups." She promised to use her powers of meditation to prevent suicides, fix broken homes, find jobs, and cure cancer. And she promised to return the money and goods to her customers. One fifty-year-old woman, who had found the psychic through a newspaper ad, forked over $241,000. "It's hard to explain," she said.

"Murder is always a mistake; one should never do anything that one cannot talk about after dinner."
—Oscar Wilde

Leaving Things Hanging

Hangmen have not generally been known either for their intelligence or their competence. For example, the famous English surgeon, John Hunter, acquired the body of a hanged man from Newgate, but when he started to dissect it for his anatomy class, the corpse sat up and demanded, "What do you think you're doing?" In Ireland, two medical assistants were carrying a hanged man to their lab, when one of them said, "Glory, Pat, doesn't he feel warm to you?" At which point the corpse said, "Yes, lads, I am a bit warm."

There was a custom in Ireland: as soon as the hangman had done his job and left, the victim's friends were allowed to cut him down and carry him away. In one case, two friends carried Mr. Mahoney of Connought away in his coffin, when he suddenly awakened and, realizing he was still alive, gave three loud cheers. Whereupon, one of his friends and rescuers hit him over the head to silence him—and killed him.

Wrong Store

In Ann Arbor, Michigan, a shoplifter made off with a pair of running shoes and a running suit that he was trying on, plus a running suit for his girlfriend. There were a couple of problems. First, the theft occurred during the Ann Arbor Art Fair, during which there were many tourists and Art Fair workers on the streets to help apprehend a thief. Second, the store itself, named Running Fit, specialized in running equipment and was staffed by runners. The sales clerk happened to be Amy Bannister, a runner for the University of Michigan and the Big Ten indoor champion at 800 meters. She chased the man down the street, gaining on him and yelling, and

Art Fair workers promptly tackled him and turned him over to police.

Invisible Man

Until quite recently, many criminals believed that any part of the body of a dead person—especially of an executed murderer—has magical properties and brings good luck. For example, in 1894 a German named Sier was convicted for exhuming the body of a newly buried child and taking one of her eyes. He was convinced that this would render him invisible to mortal sight, and thus allow him to steal things with impunity. Apparently it didn't work out too well. But he *was* rendered invisible to the public for fourteen months.

Bad Directions

One night in Ionia, Michigan, two burglars used a front-end loader to hoist a grocery store safe into their pickup truck. They escaped unseen. However, they made a slight mistake: with the 2000-pound safe in plain view, they stopped and asked a man for directions. He gave directions, all right—to the thieves, and to the police as well.

Slow Weapon

This is unique in the annals of stickups. In Balch Springs, Texas, a Dominos pizza deliverer was held up by a pair of thieves who stuck an unusual weapon in his face—a snapping turtle.

"A thief is one who considers himself honest if he has no chance to steal."   —*Jewish proverb*

DEATH

Imelda's Man

Imelda Marcos proves her love over and over again for her dear departed husband. She still changes his shirt twice a week, and on his birthday in 1990 she threw a party for him; he attended in a refrigerated casket. She topped off the evening with a soulful rendition of "Happy Birthday," sung to the corpse.

Dearly Departed

There are now on the market teddy bears that hold the ashes of the dearly departed—so that the bereaved can hug their loved ones even after they have passed into the next world.

Lord Grimsley's Funeral

His Most Gracious Majesty the Lord Grimsley of Katmandu died of a drug overdose in 1974.

For three weeks he lay in state on a posh bed in luxurious surroundings, and was then buried in a casket covered with carnations. The funeral oration included readings from the poetry of Wordsworth and Shelley. At a cost of $3,600— over $10,000 in today's dollars—it was probably the most expensive funeral ever given a parrot.

Bruce Lee's Demise

When karate king and actor Bruce Lee died of a cerebral edema in 1973, his fans weren't buying it. Some said he had died from being overhealthy—that his body couldn't handle the strenuous fitness program and a diet that included raw meat, eggs, and beef blood. Others thought that he had been murdered on orders of Chinese martial arts lords who were angry because Lee's movies were giving away ancient fighting secrets. One rumor had it that he was given an undetectable oriental poison; another, that he had been touched by the "vibrating hand," which mysteriously kills the victim two years after it is applied.

Quiet Child

The Archbishop of Canterbury christened the infant daughter of the Duke and Duchess of Chandos. Impressed with the little girl, who was loaded with rich lace, the Archbishop observed that he had "never christened a more quiet child." No doubt: the baby was dead.

Drilling For . . .

In 1971 an Englishman named William Hall killed himself by boring eight holes into his head with an electric drill.

Tiger Lady

One Lily Scramlin was an ardent fan of the Detroit Tigers. So much so, that when she died she insisted on being buried in a Tiger uniform and having her casket draped with yellow tiger lilies and trimmed in the team's colors of midnight blue and orange. The lid bore a Tigers emblem, and "Take Me Out to the Ball Game" was played at her funeral. Said her daughter, "Everything in her house is Detroit Tigers . . . When she was comatose, we turned on the ball game and she smiled."

"I'm not afraid to die. I just don't want to be there when it happens."   —Woody Allen

---

Oversize Coffin

In 1977, Sandra West, a thirty-seven-year-old woman from Texas, was buried in a huge coffin and covered over with cement. Why a huge coffin? Why cement? Because Sandra was buried,

as specified in her will, in her blue Ferrari—
with the seat tilted back.

Hearty Appetite

In 1774, a French convict from Nantes died suddenly after complaining of terrible stomach
cramps. In his stomach the coroner found a
knife, pewter spoons, buttons, glass, iron and
wood. In his report, the coroner concluded that
"it must have been something he ate."

The Sheik

When Rudolph Valentino, the movie superstar
of the 1920s, suddenly died at age thirty-one,
hearts broke everywhere. And brains too, apparently, because fans insisted on following their
fantasy man into the hereafter. Clutching sheets
of love poetry she had written about Valentino,
a British actress took poison. A housewife in
New York shot herself while cradling Valentino
photos in her arms. Two Japanese fans leaped
into a volcano. And in Italy, Mussolini himself
exhorted women to pray for the great star but
not to follow him.

Life After Forty?

When tea first became available in Europe in the
sixteenth century, some physicians warned that

it would bring an early death to those who drank it—especially those over forty.

"Die, my dear Doctor, that's the last thing I shall do!"
—Lord Palmerston

Morbidity Tour

There is now a Hollywood tour that promises to cover "more than thirty miles of movieland morbidity" at "$30 per body." It covers sites where Johnny Stompanato, boyfriend of Lana Turner, was stabbed to death by Lana's daughter Cherryl Crane; where Sharon Tate was murdered by the Manson gang; and where silent-film director William Desmond Taylor was shot twice through the heart—a killing still unsolved.

Says the tour's founder, Greg Smith, "I grew up in Kansas where nothing much happens ... When I moved to L.A., this is the kind of stuff I wanted to see."

Cure for Suicide

A twenty-eight-year-old woman in Chungho, Taiwan, attempted to commit suicide by leaping into a sewage canal. However, she changed her mind the instant she hit the water because the canal was so foul that she couldn't stand it.

Non-drinkers' Bier

After President Warren Harding died, in a courtesy gesture the Democratic convention passed a resolution that "Our party stands uncovered at the bier of Warren G. Harding." However, so powerful were the prohibitionists in those days that, to avoid offending them, the word "bier" was changed to "grave."

Serious About a Tan

One 107-degree Arizona day in 1990, a thirty-seven-year-old woman trotted out to her apartment pool to catch a tan. Six hours later poolsiders noticed that she was still there and looking somewhat fried, and failing to rouse her, they called the medics. At the hospital, her temperature registered 107 degrees, and there were second degree burns all over the front of her body. She had literally cooked herself to death.

"For three days after death, hair and fingernails continue to grow but phone calls taper off."
—Johnny Carson

LAW

Double Cross

Nineteenth-century Missouri law: "When two trains approach a crossing at the same time, both must stop and neither may proceed until the other has passed."

Tennis, Anyone?

Current laws regarding tennis:

- *Alabaster, Michigan*—citizens are not allowed to whistle while playing tennis, or within 500 feet of a tennis court.
- *Clearbrook, Minnesota*—citizens are not allowed to play tennis within four hours after eating garlic.
- *Cotton Valley, Louisiana*—no one can play tennis while wearing a hat that could scare a timid person.
- *Kennonsburg, Ohio*—a husband cannot play

tennis unaccompanied by his wife unless he has been married for over twelve months.

Hammurabi

The most famous pre-Roman law code was the code of Hammurabi, written two thousand years before Christ. The basis of the code is *lex talionis*—"an eye for an eye, a tooth for a tooth." The code carried this to such an extreme that if a house fell and killed the son of the owner, the son of the guilty builder was killed rather than the builder himself.

Kansas Pi

Kansas once passed a law rounding off the value of pi to an even three.

Animal Tales

Until quite recently, it has been usual to hold animals responsible for violating the law—either secular or ecclesiastical—and to punish them accordingly.

- In 1394, a pig was hanged at Mortaign, France, for having sacreligiously eaten a consecrated wafer.
- In 1474, the magistrates at Basel, Switzerland, sentenced a rooster to be burned at the

stake ". . . for the heinous and unnatural crime of laying an egg."

- Egbert, Bishop of Trier, anathematized swallows that were annoying the church faithful with their chirping and chattering, and which—far worse!—decorated his head and vestments while he was at the altar. He forbade them to enter the church on pain of death.
- In 1559, Daniel Greysser of Dresden was commended for having "put under ban the sparrows, on account of their unceasing and extremely vexatious chatterings and scandalous unchastity during the sermon. . . ."
- Sometimes beasts were dressed as humans before sentences were carried out. In 1266, near Paris, a pig was publicly burned for killing a child. The sow was dressed in man's clothes for the occasion. In 1685, a wolf, thought to be an incarnation of the deceased burgomaster of Ansbach, Germany, was killed. Before the formal hanging, it was clad in a flesh-colored cloth, adorned with a chestnut wig and a long white beard and had its face covered with a mask bearing the burgomaster's features.
- Sometimes people employed more humane methods for getting rid of animals. For example, they wrote them letters. In the tenth century Kassianos Bassos, a Bythnian, told how to get rid of troublesome field mice: he advised people to write on a slip of paper these words: "I adjure you, O mice who dwell here, not to injure me yourselves nor permit any other mouse to do so; and I make

over to you this field [describing it]. But should I find you here after having been warned, with the help of the mother of the gods I will cut you in seven pieces."

But this was long ago, you say, and in a region of the world where stupidity was—and is—commonplace. Then try this: As recently as 1888 a man in Maine wrote a letter to a pack of rats. Addressing them "Messrs. Rat and Co.," he expressed deep interest in their welfare, and stated that since the house at 1 Seaview Street was designed for summer, for the winter the rats should move to 6 Incubator Street, where they could be "snug and happy" in a splendid, well-stocked cellar. The writer concluded that he would do the rats no harm if they heeded his advice, but if not, he would be forced to use the poison "Rough on Rats."

"Lawyers, I suppose, were children once."
—*Charles Lamb*

Bad Rumor

The ancient Greek city of Amyclae demanded that people hold their tongues. The reason? In the past, hearing rumors that the Spartan army was coming, the Amyclaens had often panicked—so a law was passed forbidding rumors. Violators would be executed.

Eventually the Spartans actually did appear—but of course no one had the courage to report it. The city was taken without a fight.

Objects of Scorn

Law codes have not always been as unimpeachably brilliant as ours. For example, laws in many times and places have demanded punishment of *inanimate objects*. In ancient Greece, a sword was banished from Athens because it had killed a priest. So was a bust of the poet Theognis, which had fallen on a man and killed him. A statue erected in honor of a famous athlete was dumped into the sea because it fell on a man who was trying to defile it. In China, fifteen wooden idols were tried and condemned to decapitation for having caused the death of a general. The Scottish beached boats in which fishermen had drowned, cursed them for their misdeeds, and let them fall apart in the sun. Finally, when the Russian prince Dmitri, son of Ivan II, was assassinated on May 15, 1591, the great bell of Uglich rang the signal of insurrection. For this serious political offense the bell was sentenced to perpetual banishment in Siberia.

Not only inanimate objects—corpses as well. In 896, Pope Stephen VI exhumed the corpse of his predecessor Formosus, had it dressed in full regalia, and formally tried it before a synod. Found guilty, the corpse was stripped of its vestments and thrown into the Tiber river. More recently (August 6, 1888), the corpse of a smuggler was brought before a criminal court in Shanghai,

China, and condemned to be beheaded. The sentence was carried out with all due solemnity.

Evidence Evidence

A former Los Angeles County Deputy District Attorney really took her job seriously. In the pocket of a defendant's jacket she found the photograph of a child, touchingly inscribed. Afraid that this would elicit the jury's sympathy, she simply got rid of the photo. Unfortunately for her, this not-so-clever deed was discovered during the trial. The defendant, accused of shooting a security guard, was acquitted—and the deputy DA was allowed to resign.

Go Fly a Kite

In 1970, the U.S. Park Police started a campaign to outlaw kite flying on the grounds of the Washington monument. As authority they cited a law that had been written by Congress to keep the Wright brothers' planes from getting fouled in kite strings.

French Pain

For a long time there was little impetus to discover or perfect anesthesia, because the Church believed that suffering was part of God's will for mankind and therefore should not be relieved. In the seventeenth century, the French even passed a law forbidding the use of drugs to relieve pain.

Buggery—Plural for Bug?

New England's famous Puritan minister Cotton Mather records that "... on June 6, 1662, at New Haven, there was a most unparalleled wretch, one Potter by name ... executed for damnable Bestialities." Though a churchgoer and pious, he had "... lived in most infamous Buggeries for no less than fifty years together, and now at the gallows there were killed before his eyes a cow, two heifers, three sheep and two sows...."

Buggery scandalized Europe, too. In some cases, however, the animal was considered an innocent victim and spared—but only if vouched for. Jaques Ferron, of Vanvres, France, was caught *in flagrante delicto* with a she-ass in 1750. Ferron was hanged, but the she-ass was acquitted after inhabitants of the town signed a certificate stating that they had known her for four years, and that she had always been virtuous and well-behaved and had never caused any scandal; "they were willing to bear witness that she is in word and deed and in all her habits of life a most honest creature."

"It ain't no sin if you crack a few laws now and then, just so long as you don't break any."   —Mae West

---

Beyond a Reasonable Doubt?

A few years ago a peace activist named Katya Komisaruk broke into an unmanned building at Vandenburg Air Force Base and for two hours attacked a million-dollar IBM computer with a crowbar, hammer, bolt cutter and cordless drill. She got five years for attacking the computer, which she believed would be used to direct an attack on the Soviet Union. While in prison, she applied to some of the best law schools in the country: Stanford, Harvard, California-Berkeley. All three accepted her. Of 5,715 applicants, she was one of only 410 admitted. Stanford, for one, justified selecting her because they "felt she could contribute to the academic diversity of the school."

Getting Carried Away

The Incas of ancient Peru sometimes tended to get carried away. In the legal code of their ruler, Pachacutez, adultery was punished by executing not only the adultress and her seducer, but also the children, slaves and kindred of both culprits, and all the inhabitants of the city in which the crime was committed. For good measure, the city itself was razed and the site covered with stones.

Small Ban

In New York, a couple of new sports became so popular so fast that in 1990 the state had to ban them. The sports? Dwarf tossing and its relative dwarf bowling. Dwarf tossing is a sport in which people pick up harnessed dwarfs and heave them as far as possible against a padded target. In dwarf bowling, a helmeted dwarf is strapped to a skateboard and rolled into bowling pins. The sport had developed to the point at which cash prizes were being offered to the winners.

"Of course there's a different law for the rich and poor; otherwise, who would go into business?"
—E. Ralph Stewart

Lascivious Oldsters

A couple of years ago, the owner of a trailer park in St. Petersburg, Florida, wanted to evict unmarried old couples who were living together in the same trailers. As justification he cited an 1868 law against "lewd and lascivious" cohabitation. He assumed a lot.

Legal Murder

Only in 1974 did the Texas legislature repeal a 1837 law that allowed a husband to murder his wife's lover if he caught the pair in the sex act. Argentina had a similar law which was not repealed until 1991.

Dog Teeth

In 1990, the California legislature overturned a recently imposed state regulation that allowed dogs' teeth to be cleaned only by veterinarians.

Don't Bug Me

Through much of Western history, not even insects have been above the law:

- In Beaujeu, France, in 1488, the local curates warned an ornery passle of slugs three times to stop consuming the herbs of field and vine, ". . . and if they do not heed this our command, we excommunicate them and smite them with our anathema."
- During the late Middle Ages locusts were found guilty of destroying vegetation and were condemned to vacate the premises within six days on pain of anathema. ". . . we admonish . . . the aforesaid locusts . . . under pain of malediction and anathema to depart from the vineyards and fields of this district within six days from the publication of this sentence and to do no further damage. . . ."
- In 1659, in Italy, certain destructive caterpillars were officially summoned to court: So that the caterpillars would be sure to see the summons, copies were tacked to trees in five forests.
- As recently as the nineteenth century it was common in Thuringia, Germany, to get rid of

cabbage worms by going into the garden and requesting them to go elsewhere.
- In 1866, a large locust was seized in Pozaga, Slavonia, and tried and put to death by being thrown into the water, with anathemas on the whole species.

Quiet Germans

Germans have long been known for their love of order and their passion for rules. Less well known—but obvious from their preference for thick walls and stout doors—is their passion for quiet. Noise issues often make it to the German courts. For example:

- A court in Schleswig-Holstein ruled that four croaking frogs in a pond during mating season don't exceed "locally tolerable noise norms."
- A court in Bergisch-Gladbach ruled that a baby is permitted to cry unless the mother can be shown to be at fault.
- In the Bavarian town of Gaimersheim-Lippertshofen, a legal battle began in 1984 over the barking of a dog during so-called "quiet times"—usually two hours at midday, at night, and all day Sunday and on holidays. The person irritated by the noise advocated—as penalty for the dog's owner—a fine of $277,777 or a prison term of up to two years.

"I have always believed that to have true justice we must have equal harassment under the law."
—Paul Krassner

ESPIONAGE

"Military intelligence is a contradiction in terms."
—Groucho Marx

Hitler a Soprano?

During World War II, the Office of Strategic Services (OSS), forerunner of the CIA, commissioned a detailed study of Hitler's health and habits. Based on the results of this study, they bribed his gardener to inject estrogen into his carrots. Why? They had determined that Hitler was close to the male-female line, and that a "... push to the female side might make his moustache fall out and his voice become soprano." This would destroy his credibility with the German people.

Paroxysms of Madness

Another well-conceived operation grew out of the same study. It was proposed by OSS psychoanalysts based on the assumption that Nazi Germany would collapse if Hitler could be demoralized. After profiling the Fuehrer's personality, the psychoanalysts decided that he could be had by exposing him to an overdose of smut. They collected the finest library of German porno ever assembled in the United States. Their plan? Airdrop the material into the area around Hitler's headquarters. Their assumption? The Fuehrer would step outside, pick up a juicy piece of porno, and immediately be thrown into paroxysms of madness.

Fortunately, the Air Corps colonel assigned as liaison to the OSS shrinks refused to have anything to do with this bonehead scheme.

The Spy

During World War II, U.S. Army intelligence officers thought they had really scored when they recruited a French monk to spy for them. Shortly thereafter, however, the monk was caught by the Germans. Why? Because a German routinely asked him one day what he was up to and the monk, having been trained not to tell lies, responded that he was spying.

Taken to the Cleaners

In 1938, a Soviet intelligence officer named Gorin, working under cover in the United States, sent a pair of trousers to the cleaners. The pants presser had trouble cleaning the trousers because of a lump in the pocket. What lump? A batch of documents from the Office of Naval Intelligence. Calling the police, the presser not only unmasked one of the most flagrant cases of

Soviet espionage up to that time, but also identified one of the stupidest spies ever.

Hard Landing

During World War II, an Allied agent was parachuted into France one night to make contact with the underground. He was to land in an open field outside of town. Unfortunately, instead of landing where he was supposed to, he landed in the middle of an audience at an outdoor movie. The audience? A company of SS troops.

Heat Rises

During the Cold War, the U.S. surreptitiously dug a tunnel from West Berlin to tap the Soviet communication lines in East Berlin. Because Berlin winters are quite cold, some planner had the bright idea of keeping U.S. spies comfortable by heating the tunnel. Of course, the first time it snowed, the snow above the tunnel started melting because of the rising heat: this indicated not only that there was a tunnel underneath, but precisely where it ran. In this case, the U.S. lucked out. The U.S. noticed the melting snow before the Soviets did, and the heat was turned off.

"An enterprising fortune teller ... enjoyed a monopoly in the field of Western European intelligence and was even patronized by Service intelligence chiefs."
—*John Whitwell*

Soviet Backfire

When the Soviets finally did discover the Berlin tunnel, they decided to turn it into a propaganda show. Making the tunnel a public exhibit, they "proved" that the Allies really only wanted to occupy West Berlin because it was a good vantage point for espionage. The Soviets set up a beer-and-sausage stand near the tunnel so German families could make outings of their visits. However, the Germans did not react the way the Soviets expected: instead of cursing the West, the Germans got a good laugh at the Soviets not only because they had had the wool pulled over their eyes—but because they were actually *bragging* about it. The Soviets quickly dismantled the exhibit.

Cloudy Crystal Ball

The expensive U.S. military buildup in the 1980s—the one that converted the U.S. from the greatest creditor nation in the world to the greatest debtor nation—was based in part on CIA predictions about the health and expected growth of the Soviet economy. The CIA consistently overestimated the Soviet's economic strength and prospects. In the 1960s, for example, the CIA estimated that the Soviet economy was already half as big as that of the U.S., and growing more than twice as fast. In truth, of course, it was already heading into a tailspin that hasn't ended yet. The CIA continually failed to understand the games the Soviets played to inflate their economic figures. In one case, for example, the Soviets produced ball bearings. But instead of committing them to the manufacture of new and desperately needed machinery, the Soviets recycled them through the steel mills—melted them down and recast them. Why? To jack up the mill's production numbers.

Us Versus Us

During World War II there were many turf battles between J. Edgar Hoover's FBI and Wild Bill Donovan's upstart Office of Strategic Services (OSS). Hoover bitterly resented the intrusion of Donovan's new intelligence organization and resisted any way he could. For example, in January, 1942, the OSS secretly penetrated the Spanish embassy in Washington and started photographing code books and other documents of the pro-Axis government. This espionage went on for some time, and Hoover got wind of it. He did not formally protest this trespass into his jurisdiction. Rather, he had two FBI cars follow the OSS agents during one of the late night visits to the embassy, wait until the OSS men were inside the building, then turn on their sirens full blast.

"Too clever is dumb."   —German proverb

BUSINESS

Wonderwear

Every other year Honda Motor Company sponsors a creativity contest for its employees. This has produced such enthralling products as musical dance slippers, a fig tree that cavorts to popular songs, and a rickshaw whose pedals make a man constructed of papier-mâché and plaster walk ahead of the cart. Our Foolish Invention Award, however, goes to the fellow who invented underwear that is supposed to go six days without washing. The underwear has three leg holes. Each of the first three days, the wearer rotates the garment 120 degrees. For days four through six, the wearer simply repeats the process with the underwear *turned inside out*.

Gourmet Recipe

In its July, 1991 edition, *Gourmet* magazine published a recipe for mint-flavored sugar cookies. To provide the mint flavoring, the recipe called for wintergreen oil. Unfortunately, wintergreen oil is generally used to ease sore muscles. When ingested, it can cause nausea, vomiting, convulsions—even death. To correct this blunder, *Gourmet* had to send out 750,000 letters.

Nobody to Know What It Is

During the infamous South Sea Bubble in the seventeenth century, the English public went wild speculating in the stock market. They eagerly bought shares in a wide assortment of fly-by-night companies that promised to plunder the recently discovered wealth of the Americas and Asia. Perhaps the cleverest of these schemes to dupe the foolish was one started by an unknown adventurer, entitled, "A company for carrying on an undertaking of great advantage, but nobody to know what it is." The prospectus stated that he needed half a million pounds, in five thousand shares of a hundred pounds each; he was willing to take a two pound deposit for each share. Subscribers would earn a hundred pounds a year for each share. He said that more details about the enterprise would be revealed in a month.

The next morning at nine o'clock this fellow opened an office in Cornhill. Crowds mobbed his door. When he closed at three o'clock that afternoon, he had received deposits for a thousand shares. That same evening he took his two thousand pounds, left for the Continent—and was never heard of again.

Run That by Again

For people who want babies or pets but find the real thing a nuisance, there are now solutions: Video Baby, Video Dog and Video Cat. Says the producer, "This is tailor-made for yuppies. The enjoyment without the commitment." If you want a baby, you can buy the Video Baby tape and in only thirteen minutes have "the full, rich experience of parenthood without the mess and inconvenience of the real thing."

The same goes for pets. Video Dog has sold by the thousands. "You become attached to the dog on the tape," says a retiree. "Just the way it lies on the couch reminds me of my own dog." Says a camera-store manager, "I bought Video Dog for my boyfriend because he lost his dog in a divorce. We watch the tape every day."

"The buyer needs a hundred eyes; the seller but one." —Arab proverb

---

Napoleon's Organ

In 1970, a London collector auctioned off several Napoleonic relics including the emperor's death mask and a wad of his body hair—all for only $72,000. Napoleon's penis—described in the auction catalog as a "small dried-up object"—was withdrawn from a sale at Christie's because no one was willing to pay more than $40,000 for it.

Holistic Cosmetics

Cosmetic manufacturer Estee Lauder now has a line of "holistic" cosmetics. It includes Stress Buffer, a gel to be rubbed on the kidney region and solar plexus; Energy Boost, a blend of vetiver (an East Indian grass), cinnamon and lavender, which "keeps the nerves from knotting"; and Peace of Mind, made of basil, rosemary and peppermint, that is rubbed on the temples to relieve headaches.

Earthy Cufflinks

In 1969 Dino Drops, Inc. introduced a matching cufflink and tiepin set made out of petrified dinosaur dung.

Custom Furs

In the window of a Swedish furrier:

> FUR COATS
> MADE FOR LADIES
> FROM THEIR
> OWN SKIN

Yap Bread

Yap is an archipelago in the Western Caroline Islands in the Pacific Ocean. The Yaps have an odd kind of currency. Their "money" consists of massive stone discs with holes in the center. These coins weigh as much as 185 pounds and have diameters of up to 12 feet. A medium-sized coin might be worth a wife or a canoe.

Years ago, while being transported from one side of the harbor to the other, one of the coins fell from a boat into the water. It has sat at the bottom of the harbor ever since. But no matter— the Yaps have gone right on buying and selling with it.

Who's Who

Writer Joe Queenan thought he would find out how exclusive *Who's Who* really is. He invented a person, R. C. Webster, and applied to *Who's Who* in his name. The biographical data on the application included:

Birthplace: Arcis-sur-L'Abbatoir
Wife: Trish Abigail Boogen
Children: Cassette, Lother, Skippy, Boo-Boo
Education: MFA from F&M T&A University
           BA from Holy Indigents High School
           PhD's from University of Ron (Ron, France) and Quaker State University
Books Written: *Mars and Menials, Jake and Pete, Mr. Sleazy in Zion*

The mythical Mr. Webster was duly listed in the 1986–1987 edition of *Who's Who*.

"In this business you either sink or swim or you don't."
                                        —David Smith

Sterile Soda

In the mid-eighties, Brooklyn Bottling Co. was just barely making it, surviving on sales of seltzer. Then Eric Miller, grandson of the founder, took over. He brought the company back by marketing a line of low-priced fruit drinks called Tropical Fantasy. He ensured the low price by printing it right on the bottle cap, so the retailers were stuck with it. Tropical Fantasy sold well from Boston to North Carolina. Sales rose 50 percent in 1990 alone, to $12 million, and were expected to reach $15 million in 1991. Then, out of the blue, sales of Tropical Fantasy suddenly plummeted. Grocers couldn't move it. Some even stopped ordering it.

Why the unexpected turnaround?

Because a handbill had mysteriously appeared and circulated around the city:

ATTENTION!!! ATTENTION!!! ATTENTION!!!

Please be advise, Top Pop, and Tropical Fantasy, also Treat .50 sodas are being manufactured by the Klu Klux Klan. Sodas contain stimulants to sterilize the black man, and who knows what else!!!!

You have been warned. Please save the children.

Celebrity Dirt

Since 1987, Barry Gibson of Lansing, Michigan has sold thousands of vials of "celebrity dirt" dug from the yards of such illustrious people as Michael Jackson, Madonna, and Johnny Carson's ex-wife Joanna. Each vial sells for about two dollars and comes with a certificate of authenticity.

"Health" Food

A recent study by England's Ministry of Agriculture showed that so-called health foods contain more residue from pesticides than do any other kinds of food. For example, 60 percent of the nuts, beans, seeds and legumes contained traces of pesticides, as did about 51 percent of dried and semidried fruit.

"The first Mistake in public Business, is the going into it."
                                              —*Ben Franklin*

The Witch of Wall Street

In the late nineteenth century, Hetty Green, the so-called "witch of Wall Street," was considered the richest woman in the world. Her fortune totaled nearly a hundred million dollars. From her father she had inherited six million; the rest she accumulated through a series of brilliant investments in the stock market. But her brilliance in money-making was matched by her stupidity in everything else.

For years she wore the same dress. Originally black, it turned green—and then brown—with age. For underwear she wore old newspapers collected from trash baskets in Central Park. Her home was an unheated tenement and her diet consisted of onions, eggs, and dry oatmeal.

She had a son, Edward. At age nine he was run over by a wagon. His leg was seriously injured, but Hetty refused to call a doctor. She took him instead to free clinics. Because of this neglect, the boy's leg had to be amputated.

Pregnant Tummy Kit

A real business brainstorm is Dr. Stork's Pregnant Tummy Cast Kit. The cast is created by applying gauze and plaster of paris to the woman's stomach for about twenty minutes—it takes about an hour to dry. This device, which the inventors consider an ideal gift for baby showers, allows guests to "create a three-dimensional trophy for the mom-to-be, preserving her tummy size and shape for posterity."

Counting Sheep

An equally useful product is a book offered by a company in New York. Called *Count Sheep,* it presents insomniacs with 65,000 images of sheep "in convenient rows and columns for counting." There is also a handy travel edition, with 28,000 sheep. And a cassette, featuring "30 minutes of slow, methodical sheep counting. . . . You will be in never-never land well before the tape concludes."

Tough Broads

Sign in a Tokyo bar:

> SPECIAL COCKTAILS
> FOR LADIES WITH NUTS

Washington's Nurse

In 1835, the great circus huckster P. T. Barnum duped the not-so-swift public not once but three times with the same act. First, he exhibited Joice Heath, an aged black woman that he claimed was the 161-year-old nurse of George Washington. This ruse made him fifteen hundred dollars a week—a fortune in those days. When the cash flow started falling off, he boosted the publicity by attacking the whole thing as a hoax. "The fact is," he wrote in the papers, "Joice Heath is not a human being. She is simply a curiously constructed automaton, made up of whalebone, india rubber, and numerous springs ingeniously put together and made to move at the slightest touch, according to the will of the operator. The operator is a ventriloquist." People flocked in to see the automaton. But then the old lady died.

An autopsy indicated that she was not only not an automaton, but that she was only about eighty years old. Enter ruse number three: Barnum boosted the publicity once again by having Joice buried in his own family plot, and by writing a series of articles exposing the automaton fraud and showing himself blameless.

> *"How little you know about the age you live in if you think that honey is sweeter than cash in hand."*
> —*Ovid*

Some Joke

In August, 1991, an executive at Salomon Brothers decided to play a little practical joke on one of his colleagues. He got a customer to fake-bid on a *billion dollars* worth of thirty-year bonds at a government auction. Somehow the fake didn't fake, the bid went through and—surprise!—Salomon Brothers ate a billion dollars worth of bonds it didn't want.

Tourists from Erra

In Los Angeles (where else?), 450 businessmen gathered at the Biltmore to hear from Michael Horn, a 46-year-old Marina del Rey company vice president, that they should prepare themselves to receive the ultimate tourists—visitors from outer space. These were spacemen from the planet Erra in the constellation Pleiades. Only seven hours away by saucer, the Errans are nordic-style humanoids with blond hair and long earlobes. Horn showed a blurry photo of an Erran who looked like a beautiful Swedish actress with big ears. He claimed that the Errans are already visiting earth regularly, wisely overflying Los Angeles to land in the more civilized Switzerland. But sooner or later they would show up—like everyone else—in the City of Angels.

Flying High

Three Northwest Airline pilots were charged with—and eventually convicted of—flying while intoxicated. One of them—the flight captain—registered a blood alcohol content of 0.13%, when 0.04% is the legal limit for pilots. His defense? Since he was an alcoholic who had been drinking for thirty-five years, he had built up a tolerance to alcohol and did not easily get drunk. Right.

Self Service

Sign in a cafeteria in southern France:

COURTEOUS AND
EFFICIENT SELF-SERVICE

Stuffed Trump

In June, 1990, *USA Today* conducted a poll to determine public attitudes toward the controversial Donald Trump. Over 7,000 people called in. However, pollsters noticed that 5,640 of the calls came from one company. A spokeswoman for its owner, Carl H. Lindner Jr., said Lindner had had the calls made because he admired Trump's "entrepreneurial spirit."

Exalted Motives

After borrowing heavily for years, Australian magnate Alan Bond finally ran into trouble in 1990. With debts estimated at six billion dollars, he was forced to relinquish control of his empire. His antagonist in the struggle, fellow businessman R. W. Rowland, waged a vigorous campaign against Bond. Why did Rowland go after Bond with such vigor? Was he motivated by greed or by lust for power? Not at all. He decided to destroy Bond after Bond tried to take away his yacht's parking spot on the French Riviera.

New Title

Shirley Reed of Martinez, California, received a letter from stockbroker Shearson Lehman Hutton shortly after the death of her husband Ted. "We have processed your account. Old Title: Mr. Ted Reed. New title: Mr. Ted Reed, Deceased. If this new name is incorrect, please notify the manager of the branch that services your account."

"Nothing is illegal if a hundred businessmen decide to do it." —*Andrew Young*

One Good Turn

Talk about money-hungry. In Westwood, California, there is a parking lot that charges eighty-five cents just to *turn around*.

The Congratulator

There are some weird companies out there. One of them, a small outfit in Lindenhurst, New York, produces an item called the Congratulator. When you place this device on your shoulder and pull a string, a wooden hand pats you on the back. The brochure explains: "To that special employee, the Congratulator says thank you."

The Boss

The National Association of Working Women held a contest in which they asked people to nominate bosses in the categories of good, bad and unbelievable. Here are the worst:

- The owner of a retail store in Colorado who asked three female employees to shovel and rake seven tons of gravel to smooth out a parking area.
- A supervisor in a New York City service organization who kept the shades and curtains drawn so that employees could not see out the windows, and who followed female employees to the restroom and timed their visits.
- A science director at a public agency in Atlanta who went haywire whenever his secretary "poured coffee above the highest yellow flower painted on the cup."
- The postmaster in a small South Carolina town who saved sheets of toilet paper that had fallen on the wet floor so that they could be dried out for later use.

Free Crystal

A mail order company in New Jersey made over a million dollars selling free crystals that are "guaranteed" to bring good luck. How did they make so much money from "free" crystals? The crystal itself was free, but the booklet telling how to use it cost twenty dollars.

Stickup Opportunities

The *1990 Southern California Business Opportunities Guide* was truly an inspiration to entrepreneurs. On the cover was a large drawing of a stickup man holding out a gun.

Manifold Destiny

A recent cookbook titled *Manifold Destiny* teaches people how to cook food on the engines of their cars as they drive along.

"Toots Shor's restaurant is so crowded nobody goes there anymore." —*Yogi Berra*

LOVE AND SEX

---

*"Love is an ocean of emotions entirely surrounded
by expenses."* —Lord Dewar

Flowery Flop

Romantic South Carolinian Max Hedglin, thirty-
eight, spent $3000 to hire a helicopter and drop
2500 carnations and 10,000 love letters on the
lawn of his former girlfriend Bonnie. Unfortunately for Max, Bonnie had already married
someone else. Max was charged with littering.

Long-Distance Love

During the 1970s, six men from Toledo, Ohio,
forked over money for up to a decade to a young
woman they had never met. The victims included two disk jockeys, a production designer
and university students. The young woman would
call with a sob story (in one case she purported
to be an orphaned kidney patient), and then follow up with appealing letters. The production
designer alone sent her over $34,000.

Written Consent

Representative Clea Deatherage of the Oklahoma House of Representatives once introduced a bill that would require a man to obtain a woman's written consent before they engage in sexual intercourse—and to let her know that the act could make her pregnant, and that childbirth could cause health problems.

Have a Heart

Marguerite de Valois, wife of Henry IV of France, found an original use for the hoop of her skirt. She wore a wide hoop with large pockets; each pocket held a box—and each box contained the embalmed heart of a dead lover.

Gypsy Love

When a gypsy girl from Central Europe wants to capture a boy's love, she makes a nice paste of his hair, blood, saliva and nails. From these she fashions a figure, which—at the first quarter of the moon—she buries at a crossroads. Saying the words, "I love you. When your image shall have perished, you'll follow me as a dog follows a bitch," she urinates on the spot.

"I sold my memoirs of my love life to Parker Brothers and they are going to make a game out of it."
                                        —*Woody Allen*

All Wet

For some astrological reason, a nineteenth-century Parisian doctor made love to his wife only on rainy nights. After showing considerable patience, his exasperated wife finally took nature into her own hands; she arranged for the servants to pour water on the roof with a watering can. After that, it rained every night.

Railroad Babies

As recently as the early twentieth century, Moslem women in Upper Egypt aborted pregnancies by lying face down on railroad ties and allowing trains to pass over them. Conversely, women who had trouble conceiving would lie on their backs on the ties and allow passing trains to "impregnate" them.

In India, the women came up with a safer way of getting pregnant. They rushed to the tracks as a train approached, and as it passed, they lifted their skirts high.

Golden Rings

In nineteenth-century England, many women found it fashionable to wear golden rings through their nipples. Like ears, the nipples were pierced not by doctors but by jewellers. This fad has now recurred in California—and is rapidly spreading east.

Male Chastity

Do you think that only women have worn chastity belts? Not so. During the Victorian era, there was a male version of the chastity belt—technically, a form of infibulation. An adolescent boy's foreskin was gathered over the tip of the penis, and four laces pulled through it and anchored to two metal rings. This device prevented masturbation and made for painful sexual fantasies.

A professor of surgery at the University of Halle, Germany, got inventive and replaced the two rings with tight loops of wire covered with sealing wax. This allowed parents to determine whether a son had broken the seal and was engaging in "self-abuse." The good professor proposed that all indigent bachelors (those with dim prospects for marriage) between the ages of fourteen and thirty should be infibulated with wires and the wires soldered closed.

Hot Prospect

Ad in the "personals" column of a newspaper:
MALE—White, 43, ex-Marine,
ex-mercenary, crippled, triple
alcoholic seeks white woman
for dinner and conversation.

Vibrant Journey

In the mid-seventies, there was considerable agitation to institute federal control of vibrators—

to eliminate the potential hazards of using such devices improperly. Led by doctors, the movement was based on such cases as a woman in Wisconsin who came to the hospital five days after she had asked her partner to insert a vibrator in her rectum. For five hours it motored its way through her gastrointestinal system. It passed through the anus and into the colon, journeyed slowly up the sigmoid colon, and then proceeded into the descending colon, where it finally ran out of juice. Major surgery was required to remove it.

"I like a woman with a head on her shoulders. I hate necks."   —Steve Martin

---

Australian Crawl

In 1969, physicians swore that a fifteen-year-old girl in Sydney, Australia was still a virgin—even though she was pregnant. When she gave birth to the baby, the courts ruled that she had been impregnated by male sperm in the water of a public swimming pool.

Dung Forehead

Low foreheads were considered homely in the early nineteenth century. Hairlines were lifted by applying to the forehead a bandage that had been dipped in a delectable broth of vinegar and cat dung.

Naked Lunch?

Sign in a Roman Laundry:

> LADIES, LEAVE YOUR
> CLOTHES HERE AND
> SPEND THE AFTERNOON
> HAVING A GOOD TIME

RapeMan

In Japan, adult comic books called *manga* are extremely popular: according to some scholars, they are the dominant force in the Japanese pop culture—equivalent to television in the U.S. Any ride on a Japanese train will reveal many *manga* readers with their little books disguised behind brown covers. One of the *manga* heros is Rape-Man—a rapist for hire. A boyfriend who gets angry at his girlfriend—for dancing with or paying too much attention to another man, for example—hires RapeMan to ravish his girlfriend. The *manga* rape scene goes on for page after lascivious page. But how does the *manga* end? Do Rape-Man and the boyfriend wind up in prison? Not at all. In fact, all ends well. The girlfriend discovers that her boyfriend arranged the rape, and naturally recognizes it as a testimonial to his love for her. They embrace, make up, and pre-

sumably live happily ever after. And RapeMan?
On to the next assignment.

"Love never dies of starvation but often of indigestion."   —Ninon de Lenclos

MEDICINE

"I got the bill for my surgery. Now I know what those doctors are wearing masks for."

—James H. Boren

Healing Spit

In the early nineteenth century, so-called magnetic healers were very popular in Europe. For example, in 1825 a fellow named Grabe was very fashionable in Berlin—his method of healing consisted of spitting into the patient's mouth.

Japanese Virgins

Many Japanese men insist on marrying virgins. Fortunately, medical science has come up with a way to restore to woman what man has taken away. In only half an hour and for a price of $150, Japanese surgeons will create a new hymen. Thousands of *jinko shojo* (artificial virgin) operations are performed each year.

Cold Toe

Israeli scientists reported in 1972 that they had come up with a possible cure for the common cold. What was their earthshaking technique? Freezing the big toe.

Cure for Hiccups

In the early nineteenth century, English Squire John Mytton, annoyed by hiccups, tried an unusual cure. He tried to *scare* them away. He touched a lighted candle to his cotton shirt, which immediately burst into flame. But before Mytton went up in smoke with the lighted shirt, two servants rushed into the room, tore the shirt off, and smothered the flames. Painfully burned, Mytton nevertheless managed to observe that "the hiccup is gone, by God."

Semicolon

Sir William Arbuthnot Lane was obsessed with the world's bowels. In the early 1900s, he met Russian Elie Metchnikoff, winner of the Nobel Prize, who had written a book proving that the entire four-and-a-half feet of the human colon was useless: vestigial, like the appendix. This ignited Sir William. He started removing colons as readily as earwax. A boy with tonsilitis was misdirected to Sir William and had his colon removed instead of his tonsils. A man who had tried cutting his own throat almost had his *wife's* colon removed,

on the grounds that it would improve her temper
and thereby diminish his desire to commit suicide.

---

*"The art of medicine consists of amusing the patient
while nature cures the disease."*   —Voltaire

Naval Attack

Mrs. Virginia O'Hare of New York was awarded
$650,000 in a suit against her plastic surgeon.
She had told him she wanted a flat, sexy belly,
but the good doctor made a slight miscalculation:
he left her navel one and a half inches off center.

How Do You Spell Relief?

Talk about international cooperation!
   In 1975 an earthquake shook Lice, Turkey.
The English relief organization Oxfam responded
with 419 temporary houses, erecting them in
sixty days. These shelters were ignored, however, because two days earlier the Turkish government had finished 1500 permanent relief
houses—and everyone was at the housewarming.

Drugs for Dozing

In February 1976 a Guatemala earthquake killed
23,000 people and injured 75,000. Major relief

organizations—UNDRO, CARE, CFS and OFDA—did not exactly do their homework before sending in supplies. CARE and CRS rushed in 25,000 tons of food—but the Guatemalans were not short of food. Local corn prices nosedived, and farmers were ruined.

One hundred and fifteen tons of drugs arrived instantly. These included contraceptives, some tablets made in 1934, tranquillizers, drugs for reducing blood pressure, and various sample packs for American physicians. Guatemalan pharmacists tried organizing the mess, but after three months gave up, bulldozed a hole and buried the lot.

"Gentlemen, Time Me!"

Nineteenth century surgeon Robert Liston of Edinburgh invented see-through adhesive tape, the "bulldog" artery forceps, and a leg splint, and also performed the first operation in Europe under anesthesia. He was most famous, however, for his surgical speed—in fact, he was obsessed with it. In the surgical amphitheater he would challenge, "Time me, Gentlemen, time me!" He tended to get carried away. In one case, he amputated a leg in only two and a half minutes; unfortunately for the patient, he took off the testicles as well. In another case, he amputated a leg in *under* two and a half minutes, but the consequences were not inconsiderable. The patient died of gangrene; so did one of Dr. Liston's assistants, whose fingers he had cut off during the speedy operation; and a distinguished surgical spectator, whose coat Liston slashed during the operation and who thought the knife had pierced his vitals, died of fright.

Medicare

In 1987 a peer review organization found that under the Medicare program there might be nearly 900,000 cases of life-threatening treatment annually. These included about 33,000 cases of avoidable infection; nearly 2,000 cases of patients' unscheduled return to surgery for the same condition as the previous operation or to correct a condition caused by the operation; over 22,000 cases of trauma suffered in the hospital, including medication errors and unplanned repair or removal of healthy organs; and 22,000 avoidable deaths.

"Be careful about reading health books. You may die of a misprint."   —Mark Twain

---

Braless in Gaza

Modern Chinese medicine is an interesting mixture of science and old wive's tales. Recently, an English teacher talked a young Taiwanese woman into going braless. The latter's doctor, who had studied Western medicine and even taught in medical school, immediately warned her against this practice because, said he, if she went without a bra her breasts would begin to point sideways, and this would in turn affect her pituitary gland, which in turn would cause her, when she grew older, to contract Alzheimer's disease.

Finger on the Pulse

This same Taiwanese doctor has extraordinary powers of diagnosis. He can tell all about a patient from feeling the pulse. For example, he could tell that one patient had had many colds as a child, and that another had had an abortion. He also informs women that if they wash their hair in the first month after giving birth, they will have aches later in life. And that people with "cold" bodies can't drink iced drinks, and that if they drink beer they will feel so tired the next day that they won't be able to move.

The Devil's Invention

When smallpox scourged Boston in 1721, the famous Puritan minister Cotton Mather suggested trying inoculation, which he had read about in a Royal Society article. Most doctors denounced the idea, but not Dr. Zabiel Boylston. He was enthusiastic. In his zeal, he tried to excite and enlist other physicians: they denigrated him, and soon clergymen were preaching against him, claiming that inoculation would defy God's will. Boston's citizens then got mad and threatened to hang Boylston; one threw a lighted bomb into his house (fortunately, the fuse fell off). Despite this, Boylston secretly inoculated 247 patients, a group that survived at a much higher rate than the uninoculated. This didn't impress the enraged citizenry. They harassed him so much that he had to wear disguises and do his work secretly. Some of Boston's finest citizens tried to introduce in the legislature a bill to prohibit inoculation—and one clergyman, John Williams, went so far as to *advocate the death penalty* for those who inoculated. He insisted that inoculation was the devil's invention to rid the world of Christians.

Soviet Sickness

During the 1980s in the Soviet Union, 80 percent of all patients were treated in neighborhood clinics. Doctors, like factory workers, were assigned production quotas. They were expected to see eight patients an hour—which amounts to 7.5 minutes per visit. Of the 7.5 minutes, 5 were typically spent on paperwork, leaving only 2.5 minutes for the actual examination. With these enlightened policies and production "rules," life expectancy dropped in the U.S.S.R. and infant mortality rose—ranking the Soviet Union fiftieth in the world, just behind Barbados.

"A hospital should also have a recovery room adjoining the cashier's office."
—*Francis O'Walsh*

Lister's Sisters

In the late nineteenth century, Joseph Lister, father of antiseptic surgery, took over as Chair of Clinical Surgery at King's College in London. The hospital was already staffed with nurses: the Sisters of St. Johns. These formidable women completely ruled the hospital and wanted no part of this new brand of surgery. *They* were the authorities on cleanliness and the rules of conduct. They harassed Lister and his staff as much as they could. They insisted that special forms be filled out before anyone could be admitted to the hospital or even be carried to the operating theater. Many emergency patients nearly died because of these obstructionist rules. Sound familiar?

Disease Specialist

Sign in front of a Roman doctor's office:

SPECIALIST IN
WOMEN AND
OTHER DISEASES

Goat Gland Brinkley

In the 1930s, Dr. John R. Brinkley of Kansas did well enough in his practice to own a high-powered radio station, and to buy limousines, yachts and a private plane. He was so popular in Kansas that he ran for governor three times, almost defeating later Presidential candidate Alf Landon. Dr. Brinkley was also the sugar daddy of the Silver Shirts, an American version of Hitler's Brown Shirts.

How did Dr. Brinkley make his fortune? By selling a patent medicine consisting of blue dye and hydrochloric acid. And by implanting goat glands in aging men. These were supposed to revive youthful sexuality. This, for a mere $1,500 a pop—a lot of money in the 1930s. The eager consumers were undeterred by the fact that the glands failed to work.

Wrong-hearted

In Portland, Oregon, a transplant patient was given the wrong type of heart. The man had O type blood, but through a mix-up, received an A-type heart. The mistake was discovered during the operation, when lab technicians tested a sample of his tissue; but the operation had already proceeded too far to turn back. Worldwide, eight other people have received mismatched hearts during transplants. The only recourse is to replace the heart with a matched version during a second operation.

Smeared Pap

Through mismanagement and poor supervision, the New York City Health Department allowed critical delays in its clinics in forwarding findings that could indicate the presence of cervical cancer. Three thousand tests were allowed to accumulate for a year without lab analysis or notice of results to patients. When the tests were finally read, 600 showed abnormalities, including 11 with cancerous cells.

"Old people shouldn't eat health foods. They need all the preservatives they can get." —Robert Orben

---

Urine and Toads

During the black plague epidemics of fourteenth century Europe, people tried many brilliant remedies to ward off the dread disease:

- Standing in front of a latrine and inhaling the stench.
- Washing the body with goat urine (worked better when the patient simultaneously drank urine).
- Placing a dried toad over a plague boil.
- Placing pigs near a dying person so he could be healed by the smell.
- Wearing packets of arsenic in a locket, or writing "arsenicum" on a piece of parchment and hanging it around the neck.
- Breaking up the air with loud noises—such as continuously ringing bells—to dissolve the "static plague vapors." (Many years later, in the seventeenth century, this was accomplished by firing muskets and cannons.)

Secret of Longevity

For millenia man has sought the secret of long life. Apparently there is no fountain of youth, no magic formula. But there *is* an answer. According to 101-year-old Palmina Canovi, who ought to know, the secret of longevity is simple: "We're so old because we haven't died yet." Is she related to Yogi Berra?

Honest Faces

A pharmacist in North Carolina sold people drugs without prescriptions as long as the people had "honest faces."

Surefire Germicides

A government investigation of douching practices in Utah revealed that eight of the women studied douche regularly with household cleaners such as Pine-Sol and Lysol.

"Never accept a drink from a urologist."
                                        —*Erma Bombeck's father*

FEDERAL GOVERNMENTS

"A government which robs Peter to pay Paul can always depend on the support of Paul."
— George Bernard Shaw

Watchdog

The Consumer Product Safety Commission ordered eighty thousand buttons promoting toy safety. The buttons had sharp edges that could cut, paint containing too much lead, and clips that could be broken off and swallowed by small children.

Youth Employment, U.S.A.

In the U.S., the Youth Employment Agency, a financially independent organization devoted to counseling and finding jobs for youths with correctional records, over time became increasingly dependent on government grants. As it did so, it developed more and more formal rules. The focus of the agency shifted from getting good results to getting good statistics, good reports, and more grants. Under increasing pressure to meet placement quotas, counselors started weeding out the kids who needed the most help—the youngest, the least educated, and the least experienced.

Japanese Consumer

The Japanese government, industry, and courts are pretty tight—not to say collusive—as illustrated by a case against Honda in 1971. An executive of the Japan Consumers Union claimed that a certain Honda was defective; he went to court, all right, but not to get the defect rectified—rather, it was to defend himself against charges of making threats against the manufacturer.

Golden Fleece

For many years former Wisconsin Senator William Proxmire issued a monthly award, the Golden Fleece, to a government agency that had egregiously wasted the taxpayers' money. Here are some of the lucky winners.

- *Department of Agriculture*—"For spending nearly $46,000 to find out how long it takes to cook breakfast."
- *Law Enforcement Assistance Administration*—"For spending nearly $27,000 to determine why inmates want to escape from prison."
- *National Endowment for the Arts*—"For a $6,025 grant to an artist to film the throwing

of crepe paper and burning gases out of high flying airplanes."

- *Environmental Protection Agency*—"For spending $38,174 in a two-year study to find out that runoff from open stacks of cow manure on Vermont farms causes the pollution of water in nearby small streams and ponds."

- *Office of Education*—"For spending $219,592 to develop a 'curriculum package' to teach college students how to watch television."

- *Environmental Protection Agency*—"For spending an extra 1 to 1.2 million dollars to preserve a Trenton, New Jersey sewer as an historical monument."

- *National Institute for Mental Health*—"For funding a study of why bowlers, hockey fans, and pedestrians smile."

- *Department of the Army*—"For spending about $20,000 to prepare 30,000 fancy, multi-colored pamphlets explaining how to play King of the Hill."

- *National Institute of Neurological and Communicative Disorders and Stroke*—"For spending $160,000 to study whether someone can 'hex' an opponent during a strength test by drawing an 'X' on his chest."

Tarnished Fleece

Senator Proxmire himself received a Tarnished Fleece Award from the Young Americans for Freedom. He earned this award for his efforts to get the U.S. Department of Agriculture to fund a Dairy Forage Research Center at the University of Wisconsin—at ten million dollars startup cost and two million dollars a year thereafter— all for "studying what cows eat."

"Bureaucracy is a giant mechanism operated by pygmies."   *—Honore de Balzac*

Mandatory Raise

In the 1970s Andrew Bavar resigned his $40,000-a-year job with the Department of Health, Education and Welfare (HEW) after he was frustrated in attempting to refuse an automatic $1,272 raise in pay. He was informed that turning down a pay raise was against Civil Service regulations.

Death Warrant

The Emperor Theodosius II, ruler of the Eastern Roman Empire, continually signed documents without reading them. To break him of his habit, his sister put his own death warrant in front of him. He promptly signed it—without reading it.

Untuned Engines

The Environmental Protection Agency once spent 4.2 million dollars "to find out that untuned engines spread more pollution than tuned engines."

Sloppy State

In the late 1980s, the State Department demonstrated great respect for the taxpayers' dollars. In what was euphemistically dubbed a "lax" operation, the department:

- Kept millions of dollars worth of travelers' checks in unlocked cabinets and in piles on the floor.
- Allowed $59,000 to be embezzled.
- Couldn't account for $300,000.
- Allowed $15 million in travel advances to become delinquent.

A surprise audit of the principal cashier's office on August 21, 1987, showed "an almost total lack of internal control." There was no inventory of travelers checks, no written operating procedures, no controlled custody of funds, minimal physical security in the cashier's office, and improperly trained and supervised personnel. The operation was so disorganized that to determine how much money had been embezzled, investigators had to use the records of Citicorp.

"We can lick gravity, but sometimes the paperwork is overwhelming." —Werner von Braun

---

Japanese Crash

In 1985, a Japan Airlines Boeing 747 crashed into a mountain, killing 520 people. A Japan noted for its efficiency completely blew this one. It took fourteen hours before the first military rescue team made it to the crash site, despite the fact that:

- Two Japanese Air Force Phantoms had spotted the crash site within *four* minutes.
- Japan has an air-crash rescue team equipped with helicopters.
- The U.S. offered to send immediately, from two air bases, people with extensive experience in conducting mountain rescue operations at night (this offer was ignored for thirteen hours).

The first Japanese ground troops went to the wrong mountain. When a Japanese helicopter finally found the wreckage *ten hours* after the crash, it took no action because it had no orders. By the time soldiers finally reached the site, local villagers were already there.

These blunders were not merely of academic interest—there were survivors. In fact, the four passengers who ultimately lived reported that others had survived the initial impact and that "... children's voices could be heard gradually dying away as time passed."

Signatures

In the late eighties, the number of signatures it took to answer a letter received by the Secretary of Health and Human Services: fifty-five.

Expensive Stamp

In 1991, the U.S. Postal Service printed 300 million "Hubert Humphrey" stamps with an error on the 100-stamp sheets. The error? The wrong start date of Humphrey's tenure as Vice President. Because of this small "oversight," the stamps had to be destroyed—at a cost to the taxpayers of $580,000.

Smoking Ban

The status-conscious Japanese bureaucracy boggles the mind. For example, a middle-aged official would have liked to smoke a pipe at work but couldn't, since this would give the impression that he thought himself superior to his boss, who smoked cigarettes.

Better Late Than . . .

Back when Franklin Delano Roosevelt was President, Pennsylvanian Anne Bresensky subscribed to a woman's publication called *Woman's Household Magazine*. She paid half of the $2 subscription fee to the salesman, and was told she would be billed later for the balance. Later—but *fifty years* later?

The bill was mailed to her on March 6, 1940. It arrived on December 20, 1990. Said a representative in the Postal Service's Pittsburgh office: "It just goes to show that a piece of mail, no matter how old it is, is still important to the Postal Service."

"I do not rule Russia; ten thousand clerks do."
—Czar Nicholas I

Role of the Senate

Says Senator David Boren, "Congress is bogged down in a morass of detail, missing the big picture and slow to respond to our real problems." Want a reason? Even in this age of electronics when the touch of a button can record a vote, the United States Senate spends a full *twenty-five percent* of its time (forty-five legislative days a year) just calling the role.

Japanese Gaffe

In 1990, Japan's Justice Minister, Seiroku Kajiyama, made a slight international gaffe: after a trip to a red-light district, in speaking with reporters he compared prostitutes in Tokyo to black Americans who move into white neighborhoods and force whites out. "Bad money drives out good money, just like in America where the blacks came in and drove out the whites." Shades of Nakasone.

Penetration

Studies by the Government Accounting Office (GAO) and a congressional committee showed that the Justice Department's new, state-of-the-art data center in Rockville, Maryland, could easily be penetrated by unauthorized computers. This rendered highly sensitive Justice data—the names of defendants, witnesses, and informants, for example—vulnerable to scrutiny by criminals, and the whole system vulnerable to the introduction of viruses.

Driving People Crazy

Those who think Los Angeles freeways are mad should have driven in Moscow before the breakup of the Soviet Union. In the Soviet Union—which had only a fraction of the U.S. car population—as many people were killed each year in traffic accidents as in the U.S. Some features of Moscow driving:

- Left turns were forbidden except at the rare intersection that had a signal light, but U-turns were allowed on twelve-lane highways.
- Many big trucks and farm vehicles perpetually rattled around the city, because Soviet

drivers were piling up mileage to meet quotas.

- Despite poor street lighting, drivers were allowed to use parking lights only—presumably a regulatory holdover from World War II blackouts.
- Some traffic lights never changed from red. As if this weren't bad enough, traffic police issued citations to people caught in front of these unchanging lights, because there was a regulation prohibiting people from getting into situations from which there was no legal escape.
- License plates were coded to show who they belonged to—nationality and line of work. The police could thus pick up $10 bribes by citing foreigners for nit-picking violations. Three citations a year got the license suspended. But that was no problem, because the records were not computerized—one could simply buy another license.

Rich Ghosts

A census in 1987 showed that over 9,000 of the employees on the payroll of the African country Sierra Leone were "die men"—their term for "ghost" (nonexistent) workers whose paychecks are pocketed by corrupt bosses.

Nautical Buttons

In 1990, 990 graduates of the United States Navy's top school were surprised to learn that they had just graduated from the Navel Academy—at least that's what was printed on their diplomas.

Sorry, Right Number

Former Secretary of State James Baker III may have been an expert in foreign affairs, but he left something to be desired in his knowledge of the domestic populace. While testifying to Congress on the Israeli issue in 1990, he solicited a phone call from Israeli leaders by spelling out the telephone number of the White House: 1-202-456-1414. When this was broadcast on television the same night, the White House was deluged by telephone calls.

"I don't make jokes. I just watch the government and report the facts."   —*Will Rogers*

SUPERSTITION

"Perhaps there's no life after death ... there's just Los Angeles."
　　　　　　　　　　　　　　　　　　—Rich Anderson

The Unholy Bath

During the Middle Ages, one prominent test of holiness was the number of years a person went unwashed. The soul's holiness was estimated by the thickness of the layers of filth on the body.

Donate or Die

One evangelist makes about a million dollars a year in donations from his poor followers. One of his gimmicks: ask for donations in letters saying that some of those who oppose his ministry will die. A typical letter begins: "My Dear Friend.... Two of the people that raised their hand against my ministry are dead and a third one has chronic lung disease ..." The return rate on these letters is 12 percent—four times as high as that of most mail-order retailers.

Bulletproof Ointment

In 1987 a rebellion was crushed in Uganda. The revolt of the Holy Spirit Movement was led by priestess Alice Lakwena, who claimed to have developed an ointment that would protect her followers from bullets. Unfortunately, the ointment proved defective in the battle with government troops, in which hundreds of the rebels were massacred.

More Immunization

Such beliefs are also common in Mozambique. The "spirit army" of Manuel Antonio in Mozambique has also been mysteriously immunized against bullets. Antonio "vaccinates" his men against enemy weapons by making a necklace of razorlike cuts around their necks. He tells them that the magic works as long as they believe it and don't give in to fear. Antonio claims to have died of measles and risen from the dead after six days to receive a message from God instructing him to liberate people behind enemy lines.

Tough Boxers

Such beliefs are not restricted to Africa. In China, a militant group called the Boxers United in Righteousness began to emerge as a force in 1898. Their name and martial arts were drawn from secret societies and self-defense units that had spread in the prior years, mainly in response to the threat posed by Western missionaries and their Chinese converts. Drawing on spirits and protectors from folk religion, popular novels, and street plays, some of the Boxers believed that in combat they were invulnerable to swords and bullets.

Earthquake God

In the 1960s, Herbert Mullin of California did his bit to stave off the BIG ONE. He killed nine people as human sacrifices to the Earthquake God.

"Religions are born and may die, but superstition is immortal."   —Will and Ariel Durant

---

Witch Hair?

As recently as 1929, near York, Pennsylvania, two men killed a witch, Nelson Rehmeyer, and took a lock of his hair so they could remove a curse he had put on them.

LBJ's Cargo

In the so-called Cargo Cults of New Guinea, the cultists believe that their ancestors will return someday with huge cargoes of all the things that will make their lives perfect—ushering in a sort of utopian existence, a heaven on earth. The cultists thought the nineteenth century Europeans who pulled up in cargo-laden ships were their ancestors returning with goodies, which they would shortly distribute to the natives. Even after the natives ceased believing that the white men were their ancestors, they still believed that the whites knew the "secret of cargo." For example, in 1968, a prophet on the island of New Hanover in the Bismarck archipelago announced that the secret of cargo was known only to the President of the United States. Refusing to pay local taxes, the cult members saved $75,000 to "buy" Lyndon Johnson and make him King of New Hanover—if he would tell the secret.

Stripped

A young man in Arlington, Virginia, visited a fortune teller, who told him he was possessed. The seer lit candles, had the man strip to his underwear, and rubbed his body with raw eggs. She then informed him that to remove the curse, she would have to bless his money overnight. He brought her $16,000; by next morning she and the money were long gone.

Stonehenge Lives—in Nebraska

Everyone has heard of Stonehenge, English site of early Druid worship with its circle of monoliths oriented to the sun's rays. Few have heard of its U.S. simulation in Alliance, Nebraska. Modeled on Stonehenge, the creation in Nebraska is like the original in all respects except one—it is constructed not of monoliths but of *abandoned cars*. It's called Carhenge.

"Religions change; beer and wine remain."

—Hervey Allen

Flying for Peace

In the tense period before Desert Storm, Maharishi Mahesh Yogi, father of Transcendental Meditation and Beatles guru of the 1960s, stepped into the limelight with his prescription for ensuring peace by "nourishing" Saddam Hussein's existence.

"It's not necessary to deal with any madman. It's only necessary to nourish his existence ... and the next day he'll be a changed man."

How nourish his existence? By "flying"—well, not really "flying" but "hopping." Maharishi's followers employ an advanced form of meditation in which they concentrate their whole beings on levitating themselves. So far, none of them has actually levitated, but many can do the next best thing—they can "hop." "Hopping" is leaping into the air from a sitting (meditating) position so that you *appear* to be levitating. According to the Maharishi, this is an intermediate step leading to actual levitation.

The Maharishi calculates that if 7,000 people worldwide hop simultaneously for half an hour twice a day, then meditate together for another twenty minutes—that should be enough to generate world peace. In fact, he attributes the end of the Cold War to just such hopping sessions. He is soliciting funds from governments and concerned groups to support his 7,000 hoppers in creating "irreversible peace on earth." He says that "any man with the slightest intelligence can see the logic" behind his approach. Asked why no group has yet come forward with the funding, the guru said, "That is the mystery I've not yet been able to solve."

The Great Goddess

The Great Goddess who reigned over people's souls in prehistoric times is making a strong comeback with some feminists. There may now be as many as 100,000 goddess worshippers in the United States. San Francisco witch Starhawk, for example, offers a "Spell to be Friends With Your Womb." The spell invites women to light a red candle, face south and "with the third finger of your left hand, rub a few drops of your menstrual blood on the candle."

Keeping a Clear Mind

A chiropractor in Toccoa, Georgia, led a fight against local yoga classes, claiming they were a form of devil worship. He said that the classes taught people to clear their minds, which was an open invitation for Satan to waltz on in. City officials initially sided with the chiropractor, then reversed their decision, allowing the classes to take place—but without local sanction or funds.

"Some things have to be believed to be seen."
—Ralph Hodgson

Elves

In a recent University of Iceland survey, over half of the respondents thought that the existence of huldufolk—elves—is possible, probable, or certain. In fact, these little folks from the other world are taken so seriously in Iceland that highways dogleg to skirt their dwellings and farmers leave fields unplowed because the little people may need hay for their little cows. Do the Icelanders really believe in these creatures?

- On the advice of a psychic who can "see" the elves, the city of Reykjavik rerouted an asphalt path to skirt an elf-inhabited rock.
- In a nearby town, "Elf Hill Road" narrows to one lane as it passes a rocky outcropping— another dwelling of the little people. An attempt to widen the road was abandoned

when a jackhammer broke during the first day of work.

- Officials refer to an unseen rock dweller on an adjoining lot as "the old man at No. 102."
- Midwives in Iceland talk about delivering elf babies.
- Farmers talk about milking elf cows.
- Sometimes humans even fall in love with the supernatural creatures.

Being Absolutely Clear

In the summer of 1950, L. Ron Hubbard set out to prove that his "science" of Dianetics was for real. The objective of Dianetics was to produce "clears"—people who had been cleared of their emotional baggage and were in effect reborn. Hubbard rented a huge auditorium and before thousands of people unveiled the "world's first clear" who—according to Hubbard—had achieved a perfect memory.

The "clear" was Sonya Bianca. She was a coed from Boston. Hubbard allowed the audience to test her "perfect memory" by asking questions. A crucial moment arrived when a member of the audience requested that Hubbard turn his back, and then asked the girl to describe the color of his tie. At that moment, the "world's first clear" drew the "world's biggest blank."

Weak Cocktails

Years later, in 1967, Hubbard went to sea with some of his colleagues to escape what they considered an international conspiracy to persecute them. However, other governments saw his three ships as a CIA cover, and kept pushing them from port to port. While anchored at the Portuguese island of Madeira, the ships were stoned by townsfolk carrying torches and chanting anti-CIA slogans. Some of the more ardent protestors threw Molotov cocktails. Fortunately for Hubbard and company, the explosives caused little damage—the demonstrators had forgotten to light them.

Dirty Money

A pair of female "healers" approached a California businesswoman in a nail salon and convinced her that something terrible was about to happen to her because she possessed "dirty money." They offered to "cleanse" the money in a special ritual, and hand it back to her. She fetched $50,000, plus a $9,000 ring, and placed them in a black bag. The healers performed an incantation over the bag, gave it back to her, and left. Naturally, when she opened the bag the woman found only plain paper.

The Goddess that Failed

When the Kilauea volcano started flowing lava into Kalapana, Hawaii, Walter Yamaguchi proclaimed that his store—the Kalapana Store and Drive-in—would not be harmed because of his special relationship with the volcano goddess Pele.

For many days the store did, indeed, remain untouched, while nearby houses burned. When the inexorable lava finally did torch his store, Yamaguchi was philosophical. "Well, what can you do? Pele, she made me collect the insurance."

Sacred Paper

For centuries, China has spawned strange societies. For example, there was the Society For Giving Away Free Coffins. And there was the Society For The Preservation Of Papers Bearing Written Characters. The latter would be the equivalent of a U.S. society for preserving all papers that bear the printed word. The members of this Chinese society felt that since all written characters had been handed down from ancient sages, they deserved great respect. The society hired men to roam the streets and collect all loose papers that bore written characters—Imagine trying that in New York City!

"To become a popular religion, it is only necessary for a superstition to enslave a philosophy."

—W. R. Inge

Rules to Live By

Everyone knows about all of those "ridiculous" superstitions among primitive tribes in the East, and even in the West until modern times. Well, here is a list of things that were thought to bring bad luck in England—in the *1980s.*

- Looking at a new moon through glass (1984).
- Breaking anything or throwing anything away on New Year's day (1982, 1986).
- Looking at the back of a nun (1985).
- Planting parsley in a garden (1986).
- Hanging a picture over the head of a bed (1984).
- Failing to look at the tail of a piebald horse (1983).
- Saying the word "pig" on Friday (1986).
- Giving anyone salt—"Pass the salt, pass the sorrow" (1983).
- Putting new shoes on a table or putting shoes on the wrong feet (1982, 1984).
- Giving someone soap as a gift—it will "wash away" the friendship (1980).
- Two people crossing a stile at the same time going in opposite directions (1985).
- Giving an umbrella as a gift, opening one in the house, or putting one on a bed (1982).
- Taking off one's wedding ring (1981).
- Whistling on a ship or in a mine (1984, 1985).
- Seeing the back of a wooden leg (1982).

On a more morbid note, here are some 1980's omens of *death*:

- If a picture falls, someone in the family will die (1986).

- If a meal is eaten from a plate that rests on another plate, death is imminent (1982).
- Having a robin around the house brings death (1986).
- Making a diamond or coffin shape in a tablecloth as it's unfolded augurs death (1982).

"There is a superstition in avoiding superstition."
—*Francis Bacon*

ART AND
ENTERTAINMENT

"Wagner's music is better than it sounds."
—Mark Twain

Samson

The late Michael Landon came to Los Angeles because he won a track scholarship at USC. Though a scrawny kid, as a high schooler he had set a national record by throwing the javelin 211 feet, 7 inches. But somehow he got the idea that, like Samson, his prowess depended on his long hair. One day while he was still a freshman, some of his fellow athletes held him down and gave him a crewcut. Thereafter, Landon couldn't come within fifty feet of his best throw. He strained his arm trying, quit the track team, and left USC.

Blank Masterpiece

A famous painting—the Giaconda—hung in the Louvre for twelve years. Then it was stolen, and for two years there was an empty space on the wall where the picture had been displayed. During these two years more people entered the gallery to stare at the blank space than had ever come to look at the masterpiece.

Superstar

In 1931, Albert Einstein visited Hollywood and attended the Los Angeles opening of *City Lights* with Charlie Chaplin. While in Hollywood, he tried to explain his theory of light to a studio executive.

"For instance, consider Betelgeuse. Betelgeuse, one of the greatest stars in the whole system, can be photographed merely by means of one ray of light...."

After Einstein left, the executive instantly called his casting director. "I want you should go out and sign up this feller Betelgeuse, and I want you should sign him up quick. Einstein, who knows everything, says he's one of the greatest stars in the business."

Zines

There are many offbeat small magazines, or "zines," in the U.S.—publications almost nobody has ever heard of. Example: *Civil Defense: News & Opinion,* a zine that teaches Americans how to defend the nation by cooperating with invaders. Perhaps the most offbeat of the zines is *The Colleen Scene.* This newsletter, put out by a woman in California, is typed on demand—everyone gets an original copy. The contents? A description of what Colleen did that day and what she heard on the radio.

Hairy Art

A woman artist in Flicksville, Pennsylvania has decided to turn hairdos into artwork. She sculpts tiny cities and landscapes on people's heads, using materials ranging from twigs to sheet metal. One woman even had a working miniature TV set built into her do. Some customers have wigs made. One wig commemorated the wedding of a woman dentist; it contained a replica of the lighthouse where the ceremony had been held, as well as a replica of the wedding cake. Says the artist, "It's not a new hairstyle, it's an art form."

"All the really good ideas I ever had came to me while I was milking a cow." —Grant Wood

---

Unemployed Writer

Seventy-six-year-old William Burroughs, author of the notorious novel *Naked Lunch*, took up painting only a few years ago, but his works sell for $3,500 to $25,000 a copy. One of his most exciting techniques is "shotgun" painting: he places cans of spray paint in front of a wooden surface, then blasts them with a shotgun. Says Burroughs, "The shotgun blast releases the little spirits compacted into the layers of wood." Whatever it takes.

Pass on Pissarro

Thieves should take the trouble to know their business. In September, 1990, burglars broke into an art collector's house in Cannes, France and stole many paintings by nineteenth and twentieth century artists. However, many of the paintings they took were copies, and one they neglected to take was an original by the great pointillist Camille Pissarro. According to the collector, this painting is worth more than all of those they stole.

Strange Bird

As an author, Englishman John Creasey won no awards for doing his homework. For example, in his early western tales he had coyotes flying through the air because he thought the coyote was a bird.

Two Thirds of a Loaf

A park in Beverly Hills, California, sported a $250,000 piece of sculpture by the late Mexican artist Victor Salmones. It consisted of a set of three bronze figures: a girl named "Rain," and boys named "River" and "Sea." Thieves slipped into the park one night in August, 1990, and made off with "River" and "Sea"—which, according to art experts, are completely worthless unless accompanied by "Rain."

Not French Enough

Darryl Zanuck was a bit of a tyrant at Twentieth Century Fox. He put his nose into every aspect of his films, including the music. One picture was set in Paris. The main character was taking a stroll in the city. Zanuck listened to the proposed sound track and said, "Not bad. Not bad. But it's not French enough." Thinking it over for a moment, he suddenly snapped his fingers and said: "I've got it! Put in a few more French horns!"

"If my film makes even one more person miserable, I'll feel I've done my job." —Woody Allen

---

Tight Security

Two journalists in France set out to test the security of an art museum after recent thefts from museums in Paris. In broad daylight, the two walked into the Fabre museum in southern France, unscrewed a small tableau by Jean Auguste Ingres from a wall, hid the painting in a plastic bag under a coat and calmly walked out of the museum unchallenged.

Dropped Bowl

Many cities like to dress up their downtown areas with impressive sculpture. Miami is no exception: a number of years ago they commissioned famous artists Claes Oldenburg and Coosje van Bruggen to design them a nice public sculpture. The result? A $879,000 piece called "Dropped Bowl With Scattered Slices And Peels," a huge piece made of cast concrete, fiberglass and metal. As journalist Mike Clary describes it, "The sculpture suggests what might happen if a Jack and the Beanstalk-sized giant lost his grip on a pastel-colored bowl of oranges and it shattered all over an acre of downtown Miami."

Choice Colors

Are the French a strange breed? It caused a sensation in the eighteenth-century French court when the young dauphin, son of Marie Antoinette, evacuated his bowels in public. The untrained boy inspired the fashion designers to create a whole line of clothes in a new color—*Caca Dauphin*.

e.e. cummings?

It is not enough for Yuppie fashion plates to adorn themselves with the most expensive "image" attire—they're now doing the same thing to their kids. Fashion houses exclusively for kids have lately sprung up, especially in the San Francisco Bay area. There you can buy fashions made with fanciful motifs, such as cacti and coyotes, or better yet, reprints of poems by e.e. cummings. One company makes coordinated backpacks, hats, shoes, socks and purses for children who favor the "totally put-together look." The prices? For a boy's set of striped pants, shirt and tennis sweater, $110; for a holiday dress, $120.

Japanese Grace

Graceland, Elvis Presley's mansion in Memphis, Tennessee, is the mecca of King followers, drawing over 700,000 fans a year. In their inimitable passion for imitation, the Japanese are contemplating development of a pseudo-Graceland in Japan.

Interviewer: What would you change if you had your life to live over?
Peter Sellers: I would do everything exactly the same except I wouldn't see The Magus.

Japanese Ambassador

As the U.S. and China fought against Japan during World War II, the Chinese ambassador to the

United States, Dr. Hu Shih, was invited to attend an Academy Awards dinner. Cecil B. De Mille introduced Dr. Shih, but referred to him as the "Japanese ambassador." Although he corrected the mistake, the silence was deafening as he returned to his seat. Smiling, his wife leaned over to him and whispered, "Cecil, at last you have done something that Hollywood will remember you for."

Cemetery Shot

In Burbank, California, a student group was filming a scene in Valhalla Memorial Park. The scene called for a shooting, which was acted out and filmed. Unfortunately, the pistol held live ammunition, and a young actress was shot in the chest. Said the police sergeant, "Incredible as it may seem . . . they used a loaded gun."

European Boob Tube

You think network television is bad in the U.S.? Try European TV:

- One of the most popular Saturday night programs in France presents moderately well-known people seeking out their grammar-school classmates for on-air reunions.
- In Belgium, a Flemish game show host entertains by pretending to be Italian.
- The most popular show in Germany, *Wetten Dass* (Make a Bet), has featured exciting

items like a woman betting she could name over a hundred different cheeses after taking only a nibble of each, and a man betting he could identify three hundred German dialects over the phone.

"Every journalist has a novel in him, which is an excellent place for it." —Russell Lynes

---

Japanese Flatulence

Apparently the Japanese have always been a little odd. In ancient Japan, many villages held public flatulence contests. That's right—competitions to see who could break wind loudest and longest. Prizes and fame awaited the winners.

Great Record

New York speech pathologist Jerry Cammarata produced a fifty-two-minute LP record titled *Auditory Memory*. It gives people an opportunity to "conjure up previously learned musical experiences," and also provides an antidote to noise pollution, life stress, and the ear-damaging din of rock-and-roll. The catch? Both sides of the record are completely silent.

Dogged Reporter

Emmy award-winning TV reporter Wendy Bergen wanted to do an investigative piece on illegal dog fights for her local TV station in Denver. She wanted the dramatic reports to run during "sweeps" week in 1990, when the stations ratings were to be measured to set rates for TV advertising. Called "Blood Sport," the four-part series ran in April and May of 1990. There was only one problem: Bergen had been unable to get any genuine footage of pit bulls fighting. So she did the next best thing: she paid to set up the fights. But then she lied to a grand jury, saying she didn't. A jury convicted her of dogfighting. The penalty? Up to ten years in prison.

Ghost of Buckwheat?

In October of 1990, ABC's program 20/20 ran a story in which it interviewed Bill English, a fellow who said he used to star as Buckwheat in the famous old comedy series called *Our Gang*. The program had received a tip from a viewer that the man who had played Buckwheat was a grocery clerk in Tempe, Arizona. The show was filmed and aired. Only then did they discover that the real Buckwheat, William Thomas, had died in 1980.

Dial-a-doom

There is now a Hotline of Doom in—where else?—California. By dialing (415) 673-DOOM, you receive messages about "the coming end of the world." Says a grave voice, after the tolling of a bell, "Contrary to conventional wisdom, the end of the world is at hand. Doom's fundamental belief is that a number of global threats are combining to bring the earth to the brink of the apocalypse."

"Listening to the Fifth Symphony of Ralph Vaughan Williams is like staring at a cow for forty-five minutes."   —Aaron Copland

---

Lifelong Passion

In 1936, child actor Dickie Moore, an eleven-year-old, had a small part in *The Story of Louis Pasteur*. Like any active youngster, he found life on the set tedious.

"Ma," he complained one day, "why can't I go out and play like the rest of the kids? Why do I have to be an actor?"

"But Dickie," said his mother, "it's what you've wanted *all your life!*"

Black Ban

In Birmingham, Alabama, the host of a call-in radio show, Tim Lennox, was annoyed because a station employee's car had been broken into and her purse stolen. Since the thief was allegedly a black man, Lennox refused to allow any black listeners to speak on his show.

Junk Art

After a divorce several years ago, a Los Angeles collector started a front-yard sculpture of discarded items. Bicycles, toasters, rusted bedsprings, garden tools, machine gears, car parts, scrap metal ... Neighbors call this glorious collection junk; he calls it art.

Human Mudfish

Philippine tabloids make the *National Enquirer* and the *Globe* look tame. For example, Manila tabloids carried a story about a twenty-two-year-old Philippine woman who had given birth to a six-inch mudfish. She named it "Goldfish." The tabloids showed photos of it swimming in its basin, and also photos of its parents. The doting parents were even going to baptize the little creature on Palm Sunday, a plan that caused considerable controversy; but it never happened because "Goldfish" had a little accident. It was eaten by the family dog.

Number Six

Like the great philosopher Emmanuel Kant, Austrian still-life painter Max Schoedl was known for being absentminded. One day he hailed a horse-drawn cab. "Where to?" asked the driver. After thinking a moment, Schoedl said, "Number six. I'll tell you the street later on."

"I don't want any yes-men around me. I want everyone to tell me the truth even if it costs them their jobs." —Samuel Goldwyn

LAWSUITS

*"Lawsuit, n. A machine which you go into as a pig
and come out of as a sausage."*
—Devil's Dictionary (Ambrose Bierce)

Against the Highest Authority

In 1970, lightning struck the Arizona home of
Ms. Betty Penrose. Shortly thereafter her lawyer
and boss Russel H. Tansie filed a $100,000 lawsuit
against God—accusing Him of negligence in
allowing the lightning to strike the house.

Ms. Penrose won the suit because the defendant failed to appear in court. However, she
failed to collect the money.

Birth Pains

CNN anchorwoman Catherine Crier, a former
district judge in Texas, left the legal profession
partly because of what she considered unneces-
sary litigation, including the case of a woman
who sued her obstetrician because she had suffered pain during childbirth.

Gay Suit

In the summer of 1990, a young theft suspect in Florida filed a $50,000 suit against the Citrus County Jail and the sheriff's office for separating him from his co-defendant and gay lover. Said the young man: "They know me and him are gay and they're [keeping us apart in jail] out of the evil in their hearts because they have the power."

Satanic Soap

A couple in Kansas spread the rumor that Proctor and Gamble is associated with satanism—indeed, financially supports "the church of satan." As evidence, the couple points to the moon and the stars—which look like something from The Sorcerer's Apprentice in the Disney movie *Fantasia*—on the company's antiquated logo. Finally fed up, Proctor and Gamble sued the couple for $50,000 and asked the court to stop them from circulating such rumors.

"For certain people, after fifty, litigation takes the place of sex."   —Gore Vidal

---

God Bless America

A jury in its infinite wisdom ordered the New York City Transit Authority to pay thirteen million dollars after two brothers came in contact with electrified subway tracks. One of the men slipped and fell onto the tracks. Panicking, he ran into the subway tunnel and tripped on the electrified third rail. His brother jumped down to rescue him; both were burned and the brother later died. There was only one hook: both men were admitted alcoholics and drug abusers with criminal records. Intravenous drug paraphernalia were found near the victims. The Transit Authority, which said that the two were clearly trespassing, said "the public is being ripped off."

A fluke, you say? Another man, who lost an arm after falling on the subway tracks, was awarded $9.3 million by a jury. This fellow, a Mexican citizen who had been in the United States for one year working as a dishwasher, was drunk at the time of the accident. His lawyer insisted that it was the responsibility of the transit authority to "take charge" of him until the police arrived. Said the Mexican after the verdict, "God bless America."

Noisy Lawyers

A judge in Encino, California chewed out two lawyers for making a mockery of their profession. "You have by your conduct and by your positions as lawyers embarrassed the bar and the judicial system as a whole." The reason for this invective? The two lawyers, neighbors, sued each other over the noise one made while playing basketball in the driveway with his kids. Claiming that the noise disturbed his naps, kept his pregnant wife awake, and reduced the value of his home, Lawyer One sued for two million dollars for injuries to his "health, strength and activity." Lawyer Two countersued for general damages, claiming that his adversary had harassed him by playing loud rock music and by videotaping the basketball games.

Non-psychic

A jury awarded a woman psychic nearly a million dollars because the process of getting a CAT scan of her brain caused her to "lose her powers."

Talk About Debt

Descendants of Jacob DeHaven are suing the U.S. Government for 141.6 BILLION dollars. They claim that this is the amount the government owes them because DeHaven, a wealthy Pennsylvania merchant, was never repaid the $450,000 he loaned to the Continental Congress to rescue George Washington's troops at Valley Forge.

Spirit of the Law

In 1989, Jeffrey and Patrice Stambovsky decided to pay $650,000 for an old eighteen-room mansion in Nyack, New York. They put down a $32,500 binder. Then a local architect said, "Oh, you're buying the haunted house." It seems that the owner, Helen Ackley, had been seeing ghosts in the house for over twenty years.

The Stambovskys sued to recover their binder on the grounds that no one had told them the house was haunted before the deal. The judge scoffed, but later the Appellate Division of the State Supreme Court said it was "moved by the *spirit* of equity" to allow the Stambovskys to break the contract.

Aggressive Pole

A woman in Granada Hills, California, sued three companies and the County of Los Angeles because she was injured when the car she was riding in struck a traffic pole. She maintained that the pole was not designed to minimize injuries in collisions.

"A jury consists of twelve persons chosen to decide who has the better lawyer."   —Robert Frost

---

Condom Conundrum

Tamalpais High School, north of San Francisco, was delayed in its new program to distribute condoms to students by an attorney for the parents of a female student, who threatened to sue the school because the program would create potential liability problems. What potential liability? "Suppose the condom fails and the girl gets pregnant. Is the school liable?"

The Bank Robber

In 1982 John Crumpton IV and Jane Berry robbed a bank in Los Angeles. A few minutes later they encountered a squad of police and reached toward their waistbands. The police opened fire, killing Crumpton and wounding Berry. Berry sued the officers for violating her civil rights by not arresting her on a prior warrant before the robbery.

Oops

A couple in Naples, Italy, sued for damages after a car accident. But this was no ordinary accident. The couple was amorously engaged in their car in Naple's "love park," when another car hit them from behind. The impact, they claimed, caused a certain loss of control, which in turn resulted in the issue of the lawsuit—pregnancy.

Nintendo Wrist

A seventeen-year-old girl from Utica, New York got carpal tunnel syndrome, a debilitating disorder of the wrist that is not uncommon among heavy users of computers. Claiming she got the disease from playing video games for eight months, she sued Nintendo and Toys R Us for failing to warn her about the games' potential side effects.

Gaseous Suit

In a Portland, Oregon grocery store there were two cashiers, one of whom, Randy Maresh, loved to harass the other, Tom Morgan. Finally, Tom had had enough: he sued Randy for $100,000 in damages. He complained that Maresh "willfully and maliciously inflicted severe mental stress and humiliation . . . by continually, intentionally and repeatedly passing gas directed at the plaintiff." Further, Maresh would "hold it and walk funny to get to me" before cutting loose.

The defense argued that passing gas is a form of free speech, and is therefore protected under the First Amendment.

The judge had a different view. He simply said that flatulence is not covered under Oregon state law. Case dismissed.

"I can't do no literary work for the rest of this year because I'm meditating another lawsuit and looking around for a defendant." —Mark Twain

---

Stop that Thief

The estate of a Massachusetts car thief sued the owner of a parking lot after the thief had stolen a car from it and gotten killed in a subsequent accident. The suit? The lot's owner had failed to prevent the theft.

Sensitive Racist

An employee at the University of California at Santa Cruz sued a colleague for accusing him in writing of being a racist. He also sued the university because the accusation was written on a piece of university stationery. Though he has already lost his case in two courts, he plans to appeal to the state. Meanwhile, he has retired on a disability pension.

Odoriferous Complaint

In Oshawa, Canada, a worker in the General Motors plant was awarded $3,000 in benefits by the Workers Compensation Appeals Tribunal, for loss of appetite, lack of sleep and sexual dysfunctions. Why? Because his foreman on the assembly line had told him he had bad body odor.

Expensive Tastes

In 1987, two law students—one male and one female—happened to be hanging out at the same bar. The male student, Charles, tried to make time with the female student, Maia, and for his efforts was socked with a lawsuit and a jury-awarded bill for $27,500 to cover Maia's missed classes, medical treatment, shame, pain and embarrassment. Why the lawsuit? Charles' way of showing amorous interest consisted of planting a fierce bite on one of Maia's buttocks.

Annette's Pal?

In 1990 a former Mouseketeer filed a lawsuit against Walt Disney Productions because they had promised her in 1955 that she would become a "well-known artist"—and it never happened. She claimed that her career had never taken off like that of fellow Mouseketeer Annette Funicello.

Frivolous Softball

In 1984 a lawyer was playing in a softball game in San Francisco's Golden Gate Park. Unfortunately, it was in an off-limits area of the park, so police officers stopped the game. The lawyer sued the city of San Francisco for violating his rights of free speech and equal protection. Fortunately, this case had a happy ending: a judge fined the plaintiff $50,000 for bringing a frivolous lawsuit.

"A verbal contract isn't worth the paper it's written on."   *—Sam Goldwyn*

PSYCHOLOGY

"Anybody that would go to a psychiatrist ought to have his head examined." —Sam Goldwyn

---

New Use for Chopsticks

Many of Singapore's Chinese men have become terrified that their penises will withdraw completely into their bodies. In 1967, over a hundred men frantic with this fear entered hospitals. They had either tied their penises to chopsticks and hung weights on the chopsticks, or pierced their penises with wire to prevent them from vanishing.

Hitler's Kindness

French writer Alphonse de Chateaubriant, winner of the prestigious Goncourt Prize and the Grand Prize of the French Academy, sagely analyzed Hitler in 1939: "[T]he physiognomic analysis of ... [Hitler's] face reveals ... his immense kindness. Yes, Hitler is kind. Look at him in the midst of children, bending over the graves of those he loved; he is immensely kind, I repeat it."

Clean Dirt?

Frenchman Gaston Bachelard stated that "Psychoanalytically ... cleanliness is ... dirtiness."

Hot for Ronnie

Ron Regen, who runs diet centers in New Jersey, has a single overpowering passion in life: he wants to meet Ronald Reagan. Since Reagan was Governor of California, Regen has spent $20,000 and a part of every day trying to satisfy this fantasy. Though a Democrat, he has joined Republican organizations so that he would be invited to $1,000-a-plate dinners. He sends cakes and teddie bears every time Reagan goes into the hospital. He sends faxes to Reagan. Says he: "I would love to travel, take my family on vacations, but I use all my funds to go to Reagan functions. I lay in bed at night thinking up new ways to try and meet him. Sometimes I degrade myself by writing to people and asking for their help."

Off to Bed

In nineteenth century England, the sixth Lord Grantley was so absentminded that when he went upstairs to change for dinner he would often take off his clothes and go to bed.

Spite House

Arabs consider it very important to have good views from their houses. Therefore, one of the best ways to get a neighbor's goat is to obstruct his view. This has led to the construction of "spite houses"—structures built solely to block the view from another house. In Beirut, Lebanon, one such structure is a thick, four-story wall on a narrow strip of land that denies a view of the Mediterranean to all houses behind it. In another case—a clever variation—a house be- tween Beirut and Damascus is *completely sur- rounded* by a "spite" wall that cuts off the view from all windows.

"A narcissist is someone better looking than you are."
                                                  —Gore Vidal

---

Not Hungry

King Charles VIII of France was so frightened of being poisoned that he ate very little food— and died of malnutrition.

Keep the Faith, Ivan

Dr. Vladimir Dovzhenko does a booming busi- ness in Moscow curing alcoholics. His one-ses- sion cure, which costs $475—more than a month's wages in Moscow—consists of "recording" the patient. This is effected by having the doctor place his hands on the patient's face next to his eyes and on the cheekbones, and shouting, "I'm giving you an antialcohol, antidrug, psychological coding! Don't break the coding or you could die! You could be paralyzed!" After a quick spray of ice-cold aerosol in the mouth and a drink of water, the doctor shakes the patient's hand and says, "Call us in a year."

Kamikazee Camels?

Just before Desert Storm, the rumor mill went berserk, flipping oil and stock prices like yo-yos. There were rumors that:

- Saddam Hussein had been killed in a gardening accident.
- The white-robed prophet Mohammed had appeared to Hussein in a dream and advised him to abandon Kuwait.
- Iraqi plastic surgeons had reworked five men to look just like Hussein to make sure the regime didn't collapse if something happened to the real McCoy.
- Hussein had fled in women's clothing to France, where he was said to be planning to open a pastry shop.
- Iraq planned to spearhead an attack on Saudi Arabia with a herd of "Kamikazee camels" loaded with explosives and chemical bombs.

Short Hammock

How often have you heard, when someone in an organization is challenged for doing something that is obviously stupid, "We've *always* done it this way"? Apparently this explanation has been used since prehistoric times.

In the Amazon Basin on the upper Orinoco lives a stone-age tribe called the Yanomamo. They sleep in hammocks, whether at home in the shapono (tribal house), or on a trek in the forest. An American anthropologist who lived with them noticed that their hammocks were uncomfortably short—the sleeper had to rest his feet outside the hammock on the ropes attaching it to the supporting poles. The American asked why they didn't simply lengthen the hammock to make it more comfortable. They looked at him in amazement, and asked how anybody could even suggest such a thing. Apparently this is the Yanomamo version of "We've *always* done it this way."

Poor Shoppers

A New York couple with a combined income of $350,000 were such spendthrifts that one month they found themselves without a dime several days before the end of the month—checking account overdrawn, credit cards at the limit. To be able to eat until the end of the month, they used travel and hotel tickets they had earned as frequent travelers. They flew to Hawaii and stayed at a hotel with a prepaid meal plan.

> "I have an intense desire to return to the womb.
> Anybody's."   —Woody Allen

Status Symbols

Among the Suka tribesmen of Ethiopia, bracelets among the high-ranking are so tight that they impede the flow of blood, so that their hands wither and become virtually useless. Among the Suka, withered hands are a status symbol—the more atrophied the hand, the prouder the aristocrat.

Rats!

Sheik Shakhbut, former leader of Abu Dhabi, made a killing in oil, but never seemed to spend any money. Eventually he was deposed, and an inspection of the royal residence revealed at least one reason for the disappearing revenue: the sheik had been hording a tremendous fortune right in his bedroom, stuffing currency in his mattress and dresser and hiding it under his bed and in his closets. At least two million dollars in paper money had been devoured by rats.

Weird Address

Historically, the Japanese assign street numbers not by position of the house on the street, but by *when the house was built.* Thus, the earliest houses get the lowest numbers, regardless of location on the street.

"I knew that I was an unwanted baby when I saw that my bath toys were a toaster and a radio."

—Joan Rivers

Image Is Everything

For fifty years people wondered about reclusive and eccentric Mrs. Morgenthaler, who lived in a fenced and dog-guarded mansion in San Marino, California. Overgrown with trees and weeds, the property was long an object of extreme curiosity to local residents—children, adults, even officials. Now that Mrs. Morgenthaler is dead, the mystery has been solved. Penetrating the two acres of grounds, a local real estate agent discovered that the front of the expensive-looking mansion is—like a Hollywood set—just a facade. Behind it sits a very ordinary and by now quite rickety house.

Slumming

The ultra rich are now taking tours of Eastern Europe—Warsaw, Leningrad, Prague. Because accommodations are unimpressive, they arrive in private jets stocked with caviar, and are chauffeured in Mercedes and BMWs preshipped for the occasion. Some arrange one-on-one visits with locals, so they can say "I talked with a real local."

Love in New York

A young couple really missed their car after moving from Los Angeles to New York City. So much so, that they rent cars on the weekend, drive to big grocery stores outside the city and fill up the trunk with groceries. They take pictures of themselves at these stores and then go home. "Sometimes it's the high point of our weekend."

Rolex Defense

During the 1980s, Rolex watches became yuppie status symbols, like the Mercedes and the BMW. By the end of the decade, however, criminals had begun to take notice of these gleaming items people ostentatiously sported on their wrists— the Rolex suddenly became a juicy target. Some owners *really* hated to surrender their status symbols. One man was lounging in a Cadillac dealership, waiting for his car to be repaired, when a sharply dressed gunman sauntered up and demanded his diamond-studded gold Rolex that was worth $18,600. "No one gets my Rolex," said the man. "I'm sorry." They fought, rolling on the floor. In the end, the victim not only lost his Rolex, he was shot three times. "I know I'm lucky," he said seven months later, still recovering from his wounds. "But if I had to do it again, I think I would act the same."

Cheerios

A customer wrote General Mills to complain that Cheerios aren't "aerodynamic": when he threw his cereal, it veered left or right instead of flying straight. He demanded that General Mills correct the problem or give him a refund.

Lightweight Obsession

Talk about obsession! How about a Museum solely for *lint*. The International Lint Museum in Rutland, Vermont, displays lint from such sources as clothing pockets, belly buttons, dryer vents and screen windows. Free and open to the public six days a week, this exciting museum has had fewer than twenty visitors since it opened in 1947.

Trump's Man

After Donald Trump's financial difficulties hit the headlines in 1990, a diner operator in New Jersey asked his customers to donate their spare change to help out the then-billionaire owner of the Taj Mahal. The fellow placed a jar labelled "Donald Trump Fund" next to the cash register. He was completely serious. "I know it sounds stupid. But he's a good man and we want to support him."

"I hate to advocate drugs, alcohol, violence or insanity to anyone, but they've always worked for me."   —Hunter S. Thompson

---

Get Thee to a Tannery

For some, no price is too high to pay for the body beautiful. A recent study of more than 1,000 people who had had surgery for skin cancer found that nearly half continued to stay in the sun in the belief that cancer "was not enough of a problem to give up a tan."

Published in the April 1990 issue of the American Medical Association's *Archives of Dermatology*, the study found that 44 percent had not changed their outdoor activities one year after removal of their cancers, despite repeated warnings by their doctors. Further, 38 percent still weren't using sunscreens.

Wouldn't Hurt a Fly

There is a small organization in New Zealand that demonstrates against the killing of the house fly.

Mnemonics Candidate

A California woman placed stocks and bonds in a safety deposit box twenty years ago—and simply forgot them. In 1990, an "heir-finder" (a person who specializes in finding missing heirs) located her living in a downtown residential hotel in Oakland and reminded her of her securities— worth $127,000.

Harmonic Convergence

There are thousands among us who attribute recent developments in the Soviet Union and Eastern Europe not to Gorbachev and the new generation of Soviet and East European leaders; not to the abysmal failure of the Soviet economy; not to the striking prosperity examples of West Germany and Japan; but to those fateful days, August 16 and 17, 1987, when thousands gathered at various spots around the world to "converge for world harmony during the alignment of the planets."

"Roses are red, violets are blue, I'm a schizophrenic, and so am I."   *—Frank Crow*

POLICE

Blue Video

In 1989, CBS-TV in New York broadcast portions of a video that had been sitting in a police vault for six years. This highly creative tape showed a number of police officers of the Metro North commuter railroad cavorting in Manhattan's Grand Central Station. One of the highlights: a police sergeant romping in nothing but his police hat and asking a homeless man, "When did you notice you were turning black?"

Who recorded these revealing images for posterity? Who else?—the police themselves.

Passionate Candidate

Chicagoan Arthur Gloria wanted to be a cop in the worst way. He was extremely eager to take the police exam. So eager, in fact, that he stole a car to drive there, and then parked illegally to get to the exam room on time. After his arrest, Gloria said he thought he'd done well on the test.

Rich Dummy

Nearly 9,000 people were cited for car pool lane violations in Los Angeles during 1990, despite very high fines. Police keep a close eye on the car pool lane, to spot cars with only one occupant. People employ clever ruses to fool the cops. For example, a woman in a Mercedes placed a department store mannequin in the passenger seat—completely outfitted with stylish clothes, makeup, and a pair of hundred dollar sunglasses.

Suicide?

In Hobart, Indiana, local police chief Lawrence Juzwicki ruled the death of James Cooley a suicide and closed the case. Cooley's skull had been broken by thirty-two blows of a hammer. In their report, the police said the pattern of blood on the walls and ceiling suggested Cooley was alone when the blows fell on the top and back of his head from a sixteen-ounce hammer.

Said the county coroner, "After a careful review of the available evidence in this case . . . it is my opinion that further investigation into the death of Mr. Cooley is warranted."

"Policemen, like red squirrels, must be protected."
—*Jose' Ortega y Gasset*

Hero

Police were considering giving citizen Dean Gol-
dig, thirty, a good citizen award for pursuing a
drunk-driving suspect as he summoned the Glen-
dale, California police on his car phone. Then they
realized that he was the same man who had been
impersonating a police officer and pulling over
and interrogating motorists. When apprehended,
he was wearing a police uniform, complete with
Sam Browne belt, .357 Magnum, handcuffs and
baton holder. In his car investigators found a police scanner, a baton, two "slim jim" tools for
opening locked vehicles, two sand-filled sap
gloves and an off-duty badge holder.

Shot for Treason

Former Los Angeles Police Chief Daryl Gates, retired after the notorious video beating of Rodney
King by Los Angeles police, was more than a little
controversial throughout his tenure. In 1990 he
said that even casual drug users "should be taken
out and shot." That would certainly be one way to
reduce the population of Los Angeles—by about 90
percent.

Strongarm and Two-gun

Ex-chief Gates was not the only controversial
head of the LAPD. James (Two-Gun) Davis liked
to claim that constitutional rights were of "no
benefit to anybody but crooks and criminals."

Chief Ed Davis asserted that airline hijackers should be hanged at the airport. But perhaps the best example was provided by Roy (Strongarm Dick) Steckel. Steckel's men once found a kidnapped boy; when the designated mother said the kid was not her missing son, the police insisted that he was, and encouraged her to take him and "try him out."

Inmates Train Dogs

Everyone has read about how animal contact is helpful to disturbed children and mental patients. Well, until 1990, Texas was also using them with prison inmates—more specifically, they were having inmates train dogs. More specifically still, they were using inmates as bait to train tracking dogs in manhunting. Six inmates who were injured in these exercises sued the state. In the investigation, it came out that one participant in the manhunts was Vice Chairman of the Texas Board of Criminal Justice, a kindly fellow who was so thoughtful that he even presented other manhunt participants with jackets bearing the inscription, "The Ultimate Hunt."

"Reading isn't an occupation we encourage among police officers. We try to keep paper work down to a minimum."   —Joe Orton

---

One Year Vacation

When the state of Maryland took over the Baltimore jail from the city, they found at least sixty-five prisoners who had been languishing for months without formal charges. These included one homeless man who had been held for a year without arraignment—it seems that an error in the paperwork led jailers to believe that he had already been released. Said the man: "It's hell spending a year looking at a wall without a penny, without getting a letter or a visitor."

Wrong Face

A man in New York City who had never had trouble with the law in his life was surprised to see his face on television as a rape suspect. So were his friends and acquaintances: his life "turned upside down" after the broadcast. It seems that the police had shown the wrong photograph on TV. The photo had been taken as the man made a transaction at an automatic teller machine. According to police, the bank was supposed to furnish them with a photo of the man who attempted to use the bank card stolen from a woman who had been raped—but produced by mistake the photo of a regular customer.

Have a Nice Day

In San Fernando, California, a man discovered the bloody body of a victim of gang violence, and immediately called 911—"There's someone laying here on San Fernando, there's a gunshot on 8th and San Fernando. . . . I'm going to get killed! There's blood everywhere! There's blood from his head! Oh, damn. Get a deputy." The officer who took the call said, "Have a nice day," and hung up.

911

He was lucky—he got an answer. An audit of 911 calls in Los Angeles during 1989 showed that 740,000 of them went unanswered.

Urban Cowboy

Unable to steer straight, a thirty-nine-year-old man from Torrance, California, had the misfortune to weave into the parking lot of the Compton Police Department. Testing above the legal limit for alcohol, he was arrested for drunkenness. They couldn't get him for drunk driving, however, because of his unorthodox vehicle. It was a horse.

"A successful lawsuit is the one worn by a policeman."　　　　　　　　　　*—Robert Frost*

ZOOLOGY

"Do not insult the mother crocodile until after you have crossed the river." —*Haitian proverb*

Imperious Dogs

Pekinese dogs were given Imperial rank by the Emperor of China. While girl babies produced by concubines were put on the roof to die in the sun, pekinese were fed human milk.

A Rattling Good Story

On a camping trip near Lackawanna, New York, Michael Martinez found a two-and-a-half-foot-long northern timber rattlesnake. Thinking "Cylinderhead," as he named the snake, would make a "great conversation piece," he took it home to entertain his friends. He taunted the snake and stuck it in his mouth as though it were completely harmless. One night at the home of friends Martinez looked at the snake eyeball-to-eyeball and said, "Come on, I know you won't bite." Furiously rattling, the snake struck its tormentor on the lip. Martinez' head swelled up and only the quick action of a nearby zoo curator saved his life.

Electrifying Experience

New York has no monopoly on this type of folly. A fellow in Arizona showed off by kissing a rattlesnake on the mouth. After it bit him, he wired his mouth to the battery in a pickup truck and tried to electrify the venom out of his tongue.

Minding Their Pets

For forty to sixty dollars an hour, some psychics in California will divine the inner thoughts and feelings of house pets. Customers for these services include wealthy housewives, an advertising executive, a former publicist and a film producer. One wealthy woman asked whether her champion female golden retriever wanted to continue her career in dog shows or have puppies. The psychic relayed the animal's innermost thoughts on the subject: "I've seen other dogs with puppies and I don't want that. It's too confining and restricting. I want to learn more, and I want to do more obedience training."

Psychics sometimes reveal to owners that their pets are undergoing a sort of existential crisis. After a forty-five-minute session with a cat named Fanny, one psychic revealed to the owner that Fanny didn't feel that she had a sense of purpose in life.

"What an ugly beast is an ape, and how like man."
—Cicero

Japan Strikes Again

The Japanese are now outperforming the Americans in pet stupidity as well as automobile manufacture. Pet pampering in Japan is a two billion dollar a year industry. It provides for the country's cats and dogs such vital services as diapers, bikinis, matchmaking, weddings, yoga, and funerals. There are pets-only spas at which dogs and cats spend vacation weekends: the animals bathe, get blow-dried and then dine on special low-fat meals at the same tables as their owners. One department store prepares take-out meals for pets: the most popular is a $75 steak dinner of premium rare beef, unsalted ham, sausages, and cheese, with white chocolate for dessert.

Diabolical Elk

During the latter part of the sixteen century, a Swiss naturalist presented a large elk to Basel, his native city. But the good Baselers looked upon the strange animal as a most dangerous demon. A pious old woman finally rid the town of the dread beast by feeding it an apple full of broken needles.

Happy Home

In 1970 someone spotted a dog on Ruffle Bar, an uninhabited island near New York. Visible only from a distance, the dog became known as the King of Ruffle Bar. Apparently it had lived there for a couple of years, seemed quite healthy, and presumably could have lived there for the rest of its life. However, some well-meaning soul made the mistake of calling the Society for the Prevention of Cruelty to Animals. The SPCA immediately set about trying to capture the animal. They set a baited trap. Every day a police launch traveled to Ruffle Bar, and a police helicopter hovered overhead. This was done on orders: the police would rather have left the dog alone. The SPCA, however, was obsessed with catching the dog so they could "find a happy home for it."

"Cats are like Baptists. They raise hell but you can't catch them at it."　　　　　　　　—*Unknown*

Doggie Video

An outfit in Minneapolis called Made-for-Dog Videos is peddling the world's first video made exclusively for dogs. This twenty-five-minute tape, *Doggie Adventure,* is shot from the dog's point of view (about two feet from the ground), and includes a car ride, a duck chase, a pet store visit, and a cow round-up. It is billed as "a tape your dog can watch over and over again."

Pet Homes

A company named Tallmark markets ultra-fancy dog houses. The choices? American classic homes, French chateaux, *deluxe* French chateaux (patterned copper roofs, dormer windows), Royal Windsors, New England cottages, Georgian mansions, English Tudors, Swiss chalets, and Spanish colonials. Options include hardwood or marble floors, wallpaper and stained-glass windows. Prices range from a mere $1,500 to $10,000.

Millie's Outfit

In 1990, Barbara Bush was presented with a modest little outfit for her dog Millie. The outfit consisted of a pink satin quilted jacket with pearls and gold trim and pajama pants, and of course a pearl necklace to match the one that Barbara herself wears.

Snake Stories

Many Floridians who tire of their snakes simply turn them loose in the wild. Within one eight day period in Palm Beach County, authorities captured ten, twelve, and fifteen footers. In 1989 a private trapper caught a reticulated python 20 feet long and weighing 250 pounds. State officials suspect that the Everglades now abound with such creatures. Officials know that in 1987 and 1988 alone, over 18,000 ball pythons cleared customs at the Port of Miami. There is evidence that boas have been mating in the wild—an unamusing prospect, since they can give birth to up to 60 offspring at a time.

"There is something going on now in Mexico that I happen to think is cruelty to animals. What I'm talking about, of course, is cat juggling."

—Steve Martin

POLITICS

A Ford in Your Past

President Gerald Ford was once quoted as saying, "If Lincoln were alive today, he would be rolling over in his grave."

Reasons of Ill Health

Afghanistan's state radio announced in 1979 that President Noor Mohammed Taraki had resigned "for reasons of ill health." Not mentioned in the announcement were the twelve bullet holes in his body.

Good Deeds

In 1936 the Gary Cooper Fan Club of San Antonio touted their man for President of the United States. They claimed that he had already demonstrated his political ability in the movie *Mr. Deeds Goes to Town*.

Democracy Kits

The notorious Committee to Re-elect the President (Nixon) put together thousands of "Democracy Kits" to be dropped over North Vietnam to help win over the enemy. The kits were left over from the election campaign of 1972. Each kit consisted of just what a North Vietnamese needed: a diamond pin and a handsome pen-and-pencil set.

Fine Duds

Two of the Equatorial Guinean government's more notable characteristics are its formality and its unwillingness to pay its bills. Because of the latter, the captain of the ship that plies between it and a neighboring country, Cameroon, was forbidden by his boss to deliver a fleet of Mercedes on credit. After making this known in Equatorial Guinea, the captain was snatched from his ship by soldiers waving submachine guns and hauled to the presidential palace. There the president said that if the captain refused to haul the cars his ship would immediately be nationalized. Under this threat, the captain yielded. As he left the waiting room, he was handed a note saying that he was being fined $335 because he had come to visit the president without a coat and tie.

Golden Girl

In June, 1987, Ciccolina, a thirty-five-year-old porn star, was elected to the Italian Parliament.

During political rallies, she read out by rote her platform which called, among other things, for abolition of the Modesty Act under which she had often been arrested, then lifted a flower over her head and, smiling brightly, pulled down her top. In her victory performance, she regaled an appreciative audience with numerous obscene acts, a mesmerizing show that climaxed when she sprayed the first row with an "unexpected golden shower."

Ciccolina's Offer

While tensions were building up in the Middle East but before Desert Storm broke, Ciccolina generously offered to defuse the situation by making love to Saddam Hussein. "I am willing to let him have his way with me if in exchange he frees the hostages."

"Being in politics is like being a football coach; you have to be smart enough to understand the game, and dumb enough to think it's important."
—Eugene McCarthy

The Being Quayles

It is standard procedure for highway traffic to be cleared for a Vice Presidential motorcade, and so it was one Boston day in 1990. While whizzing along and causing rush hour traffic jams at turnpike entrances, Quayle used his car telephone to get in touch with a local call-in radio station, notifying them that traffic was okay because "My lane's clear."

Quayle Mathematics

Another Quaylism: *The Quayle Quarterly* published a 1991 calendar with memorable quotes from our country's former Vice President. One of the most memorable: "One word sums up probably the responsibility of any vice president, and that one word is 'to be prepared.'"

Watergate 1, 2, 3 . . .

Little known is the fact that the notorious Watergate break-in that forced Nixon eventually to resign was not the first such attempt by those clever agents of social progress. Once, the burglars got trapped in the Watergate complex and had to hide out all night in a small room. Another time, the keys they had made to get them into the Democratic National Headquarters didn't fit the lock (in their wisdom, they returned to the same source in Miami to have the keys made again).

Japanese Brawls

Until the mid-1960s, legislators in the Japanese Diet frequently resorted to physical violence when disagreements arose between the majority and minority parties. The Diet's stenographers, frightened by these brawls, demanded a pledge in 1954 that parliamentarians would not climb over their table or touch them or their notes during the battles. Since then, the pledge has had to be reaffirmed at least twice.

Vodka, Anyone?

At the beginning of World War I, France urgently requested Russia to mobilize quickly against the Germans. In response, one of the steps Russia took was to temporarily ban the sale of vodka. Then, thinking they were on to a good thing, the country's enlightened leaders extended the ban until the end of the war. One small oversight: wars are very expensive, and the sale of vodka was a state monopoly that accounted for *one third* of the government's income. As we know, an impoverished Russia collapsed into revolution three years later.

The Tsarina Is Dead

In April of 1945, with Soviet artillery pounding Berlin and Hitler's Third Reich about to fall, President Roosevelt died. On hearing the news, the infamous Nazi propaganda minister, Goebbels, exclaimed, "The tsarina is dead!" and immediately called Hitler "in an ecstasy" to congratulate him. "It is the turning point," he said, "it is written in the stars." He believed that the Allies would come apart at the seams, that America would withdraw from the war, and that Germany would still prevail. Two weeks later both he and Hitler were dead.

"No matter how thin you slice it, it's still baloney."
—*Alfred E. Smith*

Bush League

In 1990, the White House received 5.5 million pieces of mail—enough to keep 138 employees and 450 unpaid volunteers busy day and night. Two important letters from this deluge:

- A lovesick young man asked Bush to intercede with "one of the cutest females I have ever seen" by writing a letter on his behalf. "I would like to go on a date with her," the boy wrote. "The only problem is that she thinks I am weird."
- A Polish immigrant in New York offered a plan to defeat world communism in exchange for a fee, payable in advance. The fee? A mere $150 billion.

Slight Oversight

In September of 1990, three terrorists broke into the house of a U.S. general who worked at

NATO headquarters in Brussels. They were going to kill the general or kidnap him; the authorities aren't sure which because the clever fellows had made a slight goof: the general was away on vacation.

Sacred Detector

Governor George Sinner of North Dakota was taken aback when two state senators hasseled him for having a fuzz buster (radar detector) in his truck. Though these devices are legal in the state of North Dakota, the senators pointed out that he had the fuzz buster in his truck for only one reason: to evade the law. And that set a terrible example for other citizens. Admitting that there might be some truth in this, the governor said that the fuzz buster held sentimental value for him, since it had been given to him by his children. "It's sort of a sacred, emotional thing."

"Politicians are the same all over. They promise to build a bridge even when there is no river."
—Nikita Khruschev

Lots of Doe

The late Samuel Doe, long-time president of Liberia, led the country to financial ruin through a number of ingenious expedients. One of these was creation of a new Liberian coin. Liberia's official currency was the then-mighty U.S. dollar. South Korea coaxed Doe into supplementing this with a new Liberian coin, which was quickly dubbed the "doebuck." To obtain these thick, heavy, unwieldy $5 coins, Doe traded millions of U.S. greenbacks, which until then had served as a valuable source of foreign exchange. As an added inducement in this lopsided deal, the South Koreans kicked in an honorary doctorate for the uneducated Doe. The Liberian dollar, which until then had traded on a par with the U.S. dollar, quickly plunged to half its former value.

Catastrophe in Nepal?

Since the mid-70's, experts in the West have warned that Nepal is running out of wood—a commodity critical to their welfare. The World Bank warned that the country would be stripped of trees by 1995. The so-called "eco-catastrophe" made headlines around the world, and Nepal was flooded with experts and hundreds of millions of dollars to finance elaborate forestry and dam projects. There was one problem: there was no problem. It was all a myth. Satellite photos and ground surveys show that Nepal's mountains may have more trees than they had thirty years ago. Further, 80 percent of the incoming tree money went not for reforestation itself but for foreign experts and administration. And some of the other 20 percent financed intelligent operations like this: in a district east of Katmandu, one project couldn't find an area barren enough for their tree nursery, so they cut down a small forest to make room.

Jane Fonda's Home

In Texas, a Republican candidate for state agriculture commissioner accused his opponent of "visiting Jane Fonda's home"—a vicious accusation among conservatives. The opponent replied that he had not only not visited the radical actress, but had never even spoken to her. A curious columnist called the accuser's office for an explanation. Simple, said a spokeswoman. The accused had visited Los Angeles several times, and "Los Angeles is the home of Jane Fonda."

Reverse Sting

California State Board of Equalization member and former state senator Paul Carpenter, accused of refusing to discuss legislation with four lobbyists and a businessman because they had not contributed to his campaign fund, was nailed for accepting $20,000 in an FBI sting. He was charged with two counts of extortion, one count of racketeering, and one count of conspiracy. Carpenter said he knew he was the target of a sting operation, but that he took the money anyway as part of a "reverse sting." Former Assemblyman Louis Papan stuck up for him: "I would say that Sen. Carpenter was one of the most honest members of the legislature." Wow!

"Since a politician never believes what he says, he is always astonished when others do."

—Charles De Gaulle

Like Good Christians

During the mideast crisis of 1948, the U.S. Ambassador to the United Nations, Warren Austin, remarked that he hoped the Arabs and the Jews would settle their differences "like good Christians."

Fort Knox Gold

Some right wingers accused FDR's New Deal of stealing the gold from Fort Knox. In 1953, the Daughters of the American Revolution forced the first Republican President in twenty years, Dwight Eisenhower, to have the gold counted. The fort contained $30,442,415,581.70 worth of gold—exactly $10 less than should have been there. Mrs. Georgia Clark, U.S. Treasurer under the Democrats, generously sent the government a check to cover the loss.

The Coolidge Solution

Asked by Will Rogers how he kept fit in a job that had broken the health of Woodrow Wilson, Calvin Coolidge replied seriously, "By avoiding the big problems." And that wasn't all. He also kept fit by limiting himself to four hours of work a day and by taking a nap every afternoon.

German Racket

The English are known for their astute and tactful handling of ticklish relations, so it was no surprise when Maggie Thatcher's Minister of Trade and Industry Nicholas Ridley said in an interview that the European Community's drive toward economic and monetary union "is all a German racket designed to take over the whole of Europe." He called the French "poodles" of the Germans, and said that if the monetary union takes place, "you might just as well give [British sovereignty] to Adolph Hitler." These discreet comments rid the cabinet of Ridley.

Rent-a-Crowd

In 1990, high-ranking members of the ruling Socialist Party in France were invited to speak at a colloquium sponsored by Dialogues 2000, a futurist organization. During the program, a news cameraman noticed in the audience a comic actor from television. Other journalists became suspicious when members of the crowd, mistaking them for conference organizers, tried to collect the $60 they had been promised for attending the affair. It turned out that the French Minister of Tourism, organizer of the Socialist speakers, had rented several hundred actors, students and laborers to applaud enthusiastically during the speeches. Confronted, he defended himself on the grounds that he was helping reduce unemployment. Shortly after this public embarrassment to the Socialist Party, he himself joined the ranks of the unemployed.

"I would have made a good Pope!"

—*Richard M. Nixon*

Real Cause of Unemployment

Speaking of unemployment, Calvin Coolidge in his wisdom clarified the condition for all time: "When a great many people are unable to find work, unemployment results."

Ambassador X

While running for President, Jimmy Carter promised that he would not pay off political debts with diplomatic assignments—would appoint only qualified people to such posts. Once elected, he appointed Richard Kneip, a former governor of South Dakota who had been active in the Democratic Party, as envoy to Singapore. At the time of the appointment, this highly qualified man:

- Did not know that there were two Koreas.
- Did not know that there had ever been a war between India and Pakistan.

- Did not know the meaning of "Islam."
- Had never heard of Gandhi, Nehru, Sukarno, Chiang Kai-shek or Deng Xiaoping—or even of then-chancellor Helmut Schmidt of Germany or then-president Giscard d'Estaing of France.

Killing the Messenger

In the fourteenth century, Muhammed Shah was at war with the Hindus. One day a messenger, exhausted from his arduous travel, arrived at the sultan's capitol bearing terrible news: the sultan's native town had been captured by the Hindus, and the messenger himself was the only survivor of the massacre. Outraged, the sultan said, "I could never bear in my presence a wretch who could survive the sight of the slaughter of so many brave companions," and sentenced the messenger to death.

Mafia Image

In 1970 an organization was formed—the Italian-American Civil Rights League—to unify and rally Italian-Americans against their ill-deserved gangster image—one that had lately been boosted by *The Godfather* and *Honor Thy Father* and the TV series *The Untouchables*. There was only one catch. The man who started the League was Mafia boss Joe Colombo.

There's more. The League sponsored an Italian-American Day rally on June 29, 1970, at Columbus Circle in New York. Over 50,000 people mobbed the circle, waving Italian flags. Most of New York's major politicians—city and state— sat on the platform while Colombo ranted about the unfair gangster stereotype that was being laid on Italian-Americans. The rally was a big success. Colombo was interviewed on TV, honored at a heavily attended $125-a-plate dinner, and even named Man of the Year by a weekly newspaper. The League grew. Even Governor Rockefeller accepted honorary membership.

It was with considerable anticipation that the city awaited the second Unity Day, on June 28, 1971. On the morning of the rally, as Colombo moved jovially through the gathering crowd, an assassin stepped up and shot him three times in the head. So much for stereotypes.

"Ninety-eight percent of the adults in this country are decent, hard-working, honest Americans. It's the other lousy two percent that get all the publicity. But then—we elected them." —Lily Tomlin

---

MORE CRIME

Son of Sam

In the mid-1970s, New York City was terrorized for thirteen months by "Son of Sam," a serial killer who randomly selected and shot parked lovers with a .44 revolver. He made nine attacks, killing seven people and permanently injuring two others. By the end of his reign of terror, the city was in a total uproar, with people terrified to go out at night. Son of Sam—David Berkowitz—finally made a mistake and the police caught him. Shortly after the capture, the Criminal Justice Agency, Inc., a public service corporation set up to make recommendations on bail, suggested that because he had a permanent residence and a steady job, Berkowitz be *released on his own recognizance*.

Stressed Judge

A forty-four-year-old judge in New Jersey went on trial for shoplifting two watches. In her defense, she had a psychiatrist testify to how much stress she was under when she committed the crime. The causes of the stress?

- She'd had a recent auto accident.
- She had received a traffic ticket.
- She had bought a new car.
- She was overworked.
- Her husband had kidney stones.
- Her husband suffered from asthma.
- She was annoyed by the husband's breathing machine in the bedroom.
- She was experiencing menopausal hot flashes.
- She was experiencing an "ungodly" vaginal itch.
- She had a bad rash.
- She was afraid of breast and anal cancer.
- She was afraid of dental surgery.
- Her son needed an asthma breathing machine.
- Her mother and aunts were ill.
- She needed to organize her parent's fiftieth wedding anniversary.
- She had to cook Thanksgiving dinner for twenty relatives.
- She had to buy two-hundred gifts for Christmas and Hanukkah.
- She was trying to sell her house without using a realtor.
- She was suing the people who had cleaned her wallpaper.
- She had bought furniture that had to be returned.
- A toilet in her house was constantly running.

Nobody bought these hard luck stories. She was convicted.

"You can imagine my embarrassment when I killed the wrong guy." —Joe Valachi

Jesse James

In the 1970s David Allred was sentenced in Stockton, California, for rustling bees. He got three years for stealing $10,000 worth of bee-hives. Allred told the judge that he wanted to be remembered as "the Jesse James of the bee industry."

Ponzi's Scam

In a classic Ponzi scam, investors' money is never invested in anything. Early investors are paid from the money put up by later investors. In 1920 Boston, Charles Ponzi promised "50 percent profit in forty-five days" by buying postal reply coupons in Spain for one cent apiece, and redeeming them in the U.S. for ten cents worth of postage stamps. Of course, no one bothered to ask how Ponzi intended to redeem postage stamps for cash. In eight months he pulled in forty thousand investors and fifteen million dollars.

Cash Flow

Campus plumbers at California State at Long Beach climbed down a manhole to unclog a sewer line and to their considerable surprise found forty pounds of sopping wet $100 bills— about a million dollars worth. Apparently the counterfeiters of this money either became scared or didn't like the quality of their work, and simply flushed the bills down a campus toilet.

Hollywood Fake

In 1990, a man in Hollywood, California jumped into the car beside a woman, faked a gun, and ordered her to drive home. Once there, he realized that he had made a slight mistake: the woman took a .357 magnum out of a drawer and shot him four times.

Dogged Thieves

In March of 1986, Malaysian villagers near Malacca beat to death a dog because they believed it was one of a gang of thieves who transform themselves into animals to conduct their criminal activities.

Getting Rolled

In 1965, a bank robber in San Francisco made off with a good many high denomination bills, but greed got the better of him: he also scooped up two rolls of nickels and ten rolls of pennies. He stuffed them into his trousers before he took off down the street. With the telltale bulges in his pockets, this slick crook didn't make it very far.

Green Spoor

A Seattle man was arrested after witnesses saw him sprint from a bank to a nearby hotel. Arriving at the hotel, the police followed a convenient trail of cash directly to the robber's door.

Poverty in High Places

One of the S & L looters, J. William Oldenburg, was charged with bilking his Utah savings and loan company out of twenty million dollars. In 1990 he filled out a statement that he was indigent and needed a public defender to represent him in legal battles. The statement said he had $500 in cash and had not worked since 1984. He listed debts of thirty million dollars to the savings and loan, another nine million to assorted people, and a three million dollar tax lien. On the very day he made this statement, he was staying in San Francisco's Fairmont Hotel, in what many consider the most luxurious suite in America—at $6,000 a night.

"*Assassination is the extreme form of censorship.*"
—George Bernard Shaw

Having a Ball

In 1985, an Indiana woman took a novel approach to murdering her live-in boyfriend. While he slept, she dropped a bowling ball on his head.

College Credit

Many bemoan the declining quality of our schools, and this item does little to detract from the concern. A student from California State College at Northridge, and his pal who had been accepted on a scholarship to the University of California at Santa Barbara, got into a minor automobile accident with the pastor of a local church. Apparently worried because they didn't have car insurance, they later visited the pastor, intending to talk him into not reporting the accident. He refused and, after an altercation, they shot him. No one connected the murder with the accident. But the clever young college men took the pastor's credit cards and—not wanting to let a good resource go unused (the youth from Cal State was a Business major)—they went to a local automotive store and tried to charge $1,700 worth of wheel rims and tires. The credit card company rejected the purchase. Assuming that the card was over the limit, the young geniuses said they would return the next day and make a lesser purchase. Meanwhile, of course, the credit card company notified the police that someone had attempted a purchase on a stolen card. The killers were arrested when they showed up the next day at the tire store.

> "A murderer is one who is presumed to be innocent until he is proved insane."
>
> —Herbert V. Prochnow

Heavyweight Lynching

In 1916, a circus elephant in Tennessee was charged with the deaths of three men. It wasn't enough for the angry folks from the town of Erwin to kill the dangerous animal—they had to lynch it. As 5,000 people watched, they hanged the giant beast with a steel cable attached to a railroad derrick.

The Fixer

Los Angeles businessman Michael R. Goland was convicted of making an illegal political donation. Just hours before the conviction, one of the jurors, Mr. Barry Kuhnke, allegedly handed Goland a note outside the courtroom, offering to try and fix the case. Not the swiftest move in the world. Mr. Kuhnke was removed from the jury for tampering, then indicted on felony counts of obstruction of justice and criminal contempt—the first charge alone carries a possibility of five years in prison and/or a fine of $250,000.

Slick Getaway

One August afternoon in 1876, Jack McCall strode into a saloon in Deadwood Gulch, in the Dakota territory. Approaching the table where Wild Bill Hickok was playing poker, he whipped out a pistol and saying, "Damn you, take that!", shot Hickok dead.

McCall dashed out of the saloon and jumped on a horse. Unfortunately, he hadn't chosen just any horse—he'd chosen one with a loose saddle. Over went the saddle and over went McCall, directly into capture—and the noose.

Manhole Covers

In the summer of 1990, manhole covers—and storm drain gratings and catch-basin covers—began mysteriously disappearing from around Los Angeles. This went on steadily for nine days. Apparently the enterprising thieves thought that these items would not be missed, or that the police would be able to figure out that there are very few places in LA to unload that much iron. The culprits were caught at—where else?—a scrap metal yard in downtown LA. The heavy metal the canny thieves had stolen is worth only three cents a pound. They could have made thirty times as much—legally—by recycling aluminum soft-drink cans.

"It is a rather pleasant experience to be alone in a bank at night." —Bank robber Willie Sutton

---

Benny the Bungler

Benny "The Bungler" Puchetti, a Mafia hit man, never killed anyone. In a series of abortive attempts he:

- Forgot to load his gun.
- Slipped and hit his head on the bathtub while trying to choke someone in a shower.
- Tripped and fell on his own knife.
- Drove off a cliff while trying to force someone from the road.

Perils of Congress

In 1990, Representative Gerry Studds, fifty-three, was beaten up on a street corner near his residence in the DuPont Circle area of Washington D.C. Two men knocked Studds down and then punched and kicked him in the body and head. Apprehended later, the two fine American citizens said they had no particular motive, it was just "something to do at the time."

Botanical Felons

Why would anyone in the world want to assault a tree?

A forty-six-year-old Texan tried to poison the Treaty Oak, a five-hundred-year-old giant oak under which Stephen F. Austin signed a treaty with the Indians in the 1820s. The tree was severely damaged by the herbicide Velpar. And this is not an isolated case: an unknown vandal in Carmel, California, cut, nailed and poisoned three rare Monterey cypress trees on the beach walkway along Scenic Drive. The vandal drilled fifteen holes into the trees and filled them with herbicide, cut them with a handsaw, and drove copper nails into their trunks.

Lunch Errand

A thirty-seven-year-old bank teller in Norwalk, Connecticut punched out at lunch time, robbed a rival bank, went home and left the money, then returned to his own bank and punched back in.

Hot Stuff

Two clever thieves tried to steal copper wire from an electric transformer in Santa Clarita, California. They made only one slight blunder: they neglected to shut off the power. Both wound up in the burn unit of a local hospital.

Babysitting Bandit

A young man in Calgary, Canada attempted to rob a grocery store. Apparently the robbery wasn't too well planned. His weapon was a can opener, which didn't exactly terrorize the clerk. And he was wheeling a sixteen-month-old baby—which kept falling out of the carriage as the robber attempted his escape.

"When I was kidnapped, my parents snapped into action. They rented out my room." —Woody Allen

---

SCIENCE AND TECHNOLOGY

"A new scientific truth does not triumph by convincing its opponents, but rather because its opponents die. . . ."   —Max Planck

---

A Tail of Danger

When Halley's Comet swung close to earth in 1910, a group of French scientists published a paper saying that the earth would be poisoned by fumes from the comet's tail. The public eagerly bought up "anticomet" pills that guaranteed protection from the noxious fumes.

Scientific Evidence

In his book *Sexual Science*, written in 1870, Orson Squire Fowler wrote: "Twins and triplets undoubtedly originate in second and third copulations, immediately following the first, each drawing and then impregnating an egg. The fact that twins are born as soon as possible after each other supports this view."

Japanese Intestines

The Japanese are convinced that they are unique—not only in culture, but also *physically*. A prominent Japanese, Iwamochi Shizuma, once explained before an audience of foreign correspondents that American beef was not suitable for digestion by the Japanese because Japanese intestines are about a meter longer than those of foreigners.

New Specs

Early in the seventeenth century, stargazer Father Scheiner of Germany saw spots on the sun. Apprised of this, his superior in the church said, "You are mistaken, my son. I have studied Aristotle and he nowhere mentions spots. Try changing your spectacles."

"The great tragedy of science—the slaying of a beautiful hypothesis by an ugly fact."

—*T.H. Huxley*

Mad Mayer

On an 1841 voyage to the East Indies, German doctor Louis Mayer noticed that in the tropics venous blood appeared bright red, rather than bluish red as in colder climates. This got him thinking about combustion of food in the body, which in turn led him to a great scientific discovery: the conservation of energy. He wrote a paper on the subject and on his return to Germany had it published. It received little attention. Other people started putting forward similar ideas. Mayer wrote other papers, claiming priority for his work, but nobody would publish them. He resorted to writing an article in the newspaper, for which he was thoroughly ridiculed. He became so upset by this that he was put into a mental home. "The doctors found that his chief sympton was an obsession that he had discovered a great scientific principle and that no one else would recognize this. He was treated like a lunatic and put in a straitjacket."

Hairy Eyeballs

In 1932, William Murray, Governor of Oklahoma, stated: "It's a scientific fact that if you shave your moustache, you weaken your eyes."

Fast Martians

On August 27, 1911, the *New York Times* announced: MARTIANS BUILD TWO IMMENSE CANALS IN TWO YEARS. Vast Engineering Works Accomplished in an Incredibly Short Time by Our Planetary Neighbors.

"Invention is the mother of necessity."
—Thorstein Veblen

Crazy Legs

The famous anatomist Andreas Vesalius, who lived in the sixteenth century, started out as a Professor of Anatomy at the University of Padua (Italy) at the age of twenty-three. He discovered some two hundred anatomical errors made by the great Roman physician Galen, whose authority in such matters was virtually undisputed even fourteen hundred years after his death. Vesalius showed, for example, that the human thigh bones are straight and not—as Galen had contended—curved like those of a dog. Upset by this lack of respect for the great Galen, one of Vesalius' former teachers insisted that the human thighbone is normally curved—that the straight bones of the day were an anomaly caused by the then-fashionable *narrow trousers*.

Pinned

American Walter Hunt, a mid nineteenth-century inventor, created the safety pin in three hours and sold the patent rights for four hundred dollars to repay a fifteen dollar debt.

Stop!

The first practical pair of roller skates was built in 1759 by Belgian master violinist and musical instrument maker Joseph Merlin. Each skate had only two wheels, aligned along the center of the shoe like today's roller blades. Merlin constructed the skates in order to make a spectacular entrance at a costume party in the Belgian city of Huy. The crude design, which strapped to the feet, was based on the ice skates of the day.

Merlin planned to roll into the party while playing his violin. Unfortunately, he had neglected to master the fine art of stopping on skates. He rolled right through the party and crashed into a full-length mirror, breaking both it and his violin. There's little question that he made a spectacular entrance.

Eisenhower went into a room full of computers and asked, "Is there a God?" The computers all started up, lights flashed, wheels turned, and after a while a voice said, "Now there is."

Zambian Astronauts

In the 1960s, the United States embarked on a crash program to put a man on the moon before the end of the decade. Though little publicized, the African country of Zambia was even more ambitious. In 1964, Edward Mukaka Nkolosa,

Director-General of Zambia's National Academy of Space Research, said: "I'll have my first Zambian astronaut on the moon by 1965 . . . [w]e are using my own firing system, derived from the catapult. . . . I'm getting [my astronauts] . . . acclimatised to space travel by placing them in my space capsule every day. It's a forty-gallon oil drum in which they sit, and I then roll them down a hill. This gives them the feeling of rushing through space. I also make them swing from the end of a long rope. When they reach the highest point, I cut the rope—this produces the feeling of free fall."

Twenty years later—in 1984—Nkoloso was questioned about his space program's lack of progress. He placed much of the blame on "trouble" with his "space-men and space-women." "They won't concentrate on space flight," he said.

The Golden Arm

Here's a great invention that never quite made it. Developed fifty years ago, it was a turn signal called Arm-A-Lite. When the driver of a car stuck his arm out the window to signal a turn, his arm would automatically hit a light switch, which would "throw a beam on his arm, making it visible."

"I'm astounded by people who want to 'know' the universe when it's hard enough to find your way around Chinatown."   —*Woody Allen*

MARRIAGE AND FAMILY

"Somewhere on this globe, every ten seconds, there is a woman giving birth to a child. She must be found and stopped."
—Sam Levenson

A Pillar of Strength

In a 1976 ceremony witnessed by more than twenty people, a Los Angeles secretary officially married a fifty-pound rock.

All Fired Up

Among the Pathans of northwest Pakistan, tradition calls for a groom's kinsmen to serenade the bride by firing their rifles into the air. The Afghanistan war, however, brought to Pakistan more exotic weapons than the traditional rifle. The new weapons include automatic rifles and rocket launchers. The Soviet Kalashnikov is especially popular: it can be rented for as little as the use of a water buffalo for a day. The modern weapons make for very dramatic weddings.

In one incident, automatic rifle fire cut a high

179

tension wire above a wedding party; the wire whipped into the crowd, starting fires and electrocuting eight people. In another incident, tracer gunfire prevented an airplane from landing on its proper runway; trying to land on a road, the pilot crashed, killing thirteen people. One local doctor treats two or three people a week who have been hit by stray bullets.

Tear Jerker

The eighteenth-century German tended to be somewhat overrefined in feeling—witness Goethe's *Sorrows of Young Werther,* which triggered a good many suicides. An extreme example is a fellow named Kotzbue who, stopping at Weimar on his way to Paris, was told by his wife's doctor that she was dying. Did he turn back? Nothing of the sort. He continued his trip because he said it would break his heart to be present at the death of his beloved.

One Wife, One Bath

Until quite recently, a Bulgarian woman was permitted only one bath in her lifetime—on the day before her wedding.

Bike Wedding

Mark Warner got married in Plainsville, Connecticut, in the late 1970s. A hundred of his friends attended the wedding. After the ceremony, his bride reversed the usual procedure by carrying Warner to the threshold of a cafe for the wedding reception. That was unusual enough, but not as unusual as the bride—Warner married his motorcycle.

Children Not Allowed

Sign in a German maternity ward:

> NO CHILDREN
> ALLOWED IN THE
> MATERNITY WARDS

Civilized Divorce

A carpenter from Concord, California, served divorce papers on his wife after twelve years of marriage. The husband's lawyer handed the wife the papers, and seven friends served as witnesses. After the wife took the papers, the couple joined hands and kissed goodbye.

What's so odd about this?

The whole ceremony took place during a multiperson free-fall parachute jump from 12,500 feet.

"The woman cries before the wedding; the man afterward."   *—Polish proverb*

The More the Merrier

In 1922, Theresa Vaughn went on trial in Sheffield, England. She was accused of bigamy. She had entered into sixty-one marriages in five years while still legally married to her first husband. And all by the ripe old age of twenty-four.

Switch

In New York City, a man dying of cancer had his sperm stored in a Manhattan sperm bank so that his wife could be artificially inseminated after he died. He did and she was, and in 1990 she gave birth to a healthy baby. There was only one problem: the baby was the wrong color—black. The bank had mixed up the sperm containers.

Miscookulation

A thirty-two-year-old woman in Newhall, California, got mad at her husband and decided to burn his clothes. Where? In the outdoor barbeque, of course. She took an armful of clothes to the barbeque on the porch and ignited them with lighter fluid. Unfortunately for her, the fire decided to burn *her* clothes as well, and soon she rushed out into the street with her garments on fire. Meanwhile, unattended, the barbeque went to work on the porch, and ended up causing $40,000 damage to the house.

Rose Bowl Baby

When a woman informed her husband that she was due to have their second child on January 1, 1990, he said, "Gee, that's tough, because I've already ordered tickets for the Rose Bowl game." After intense negotiation, he finally made a concession: if his wife was in labor at his departure time, he would stay. Otherwise, he was out of there.

Attention

In August 1990, Los Angeles police discovered the blood-stained automobile of three missing women—a thirty-eight-year-old mother, her daughter, and the daughter's friend. Contents of purses were scattered in the car, the keys were still in the ignition, and blood was splattered on the seat. The women had last been seen leaving a print shop where the mother worked. The Rialto and California state police searched intensively for several days before being informed that the three women were alive and well in Utah—they had staged the "abduction" to get sympathy from their families.

Childbirth Prohibited?

Sign in a Norwegian cocktail lounge:

LADIES ARE REQUESTED
NOT TO HAVE CHILDREN
IN THE BAR

Compost Wedding

Want romance? How about a nice wedding on top of a compost heap. In 1990, Jim Norman and Patsy Stipe got married on top of the compost pile of Zeke the Sheik in Altadena, California. This is the same heap that the county had threatened to bulldoze as a health hazard, and that had spontaneously burst into flames twice in the months before the wedding.

"Husbands are like fires. They go out if unattended."
—Zsa Zsa Gabor

Aerial Gift

In 1990, a young married man bought his wife two rings—diamond and emerald—on their anniversary. Considering it too unromantic simply to hand her the rings, he came up with the bright idea of attaching them to balloons. He bought some helium-filled balloons, attached the rings, and—what else?—on the way home inadvertently let go of the balloons. Anybody find a couple of nice rings? There's a reward.

Filial Piety

The Chinese are known to respect their parents, but this is ridiculous. A Chinese fellow had a mean stepmother. In spite of the fact that she treated him so badly, he would do anything for her. For example, she loved fish, so one day he lay down naked on a frozen lake, melted a hole with his body heat and caught her the two carp that came up for air. Another fellow slept naked so that all the mosquitoes would bite him and leave his parents alone. Still another dressed in baby clothes and crawled on the floor, to trick his ninety-year-old parents into thinking they were still young.

Empathy Belly

There is now a product on the market that allows would-be fathers to know how it feels to be pregnant. This is a thirty-three-pound "empathy belly" that they can strap on and wear around the house. And to work?

Doting Mother

This one caught a lot of publicity and eventually led to a made-for-TV movie. Wanda Webb Holloway, of Channelview, Texas, a Houston suburb, asked her former brother-in-law to find someone to either kidnap or kill another Channelview woman. Why? Because the woman was the mother of a girl who in the past had beaten out Holloway's daughter for the junior high school cheerleading team—and she wanted to make sure it didn't happen again. Holloway figured that the mother's death or disappearance would cause the rival to drop out of the cheer-leading competition, and thus open the way for her own daughter. Holloway was awarded fifteen years to contemplate the importance of cheer-leading in the great scheme of things.

"Last time I tried to make love to my wife nothing was happening, so I said to her, 'What's the matter, you can't think of anybody either?' "
—*Rodney Dangerfield*

STATE AND LOCAL GOVERNMENT

"The business of the government is to keep the government out of business—that is, unless business needs government aid." —Will Rogers

---

Painful Welcome

In San Jose, California, workers had to pull down a thirty-foot banner intended for a ceremony at the public library after discovering that a greeting in a Philippine language did not mean "You Are Welcome." It meant "You Are Circumcised."

Getting Together

In the mid eighties the city of Chicago joined with the State of Illinois to build a two million dollar pedway that would connect City Hall to the State of Illinois Center across the street. The city workers started from City Hall and the state workers from the Center. Unfortunately, when the two came together in June of 1989 there was a glitch: the state's section came out nine inches

187

lower than the city's and eight inches farther east.

Home-wrecker

In 1989, Cleveland Bailey of North Little Rock, Arkansas, went out of town, leaving his house temporarily unoccupied. When he returned two weeks later, his house was no longer there. Just moments before he arrived, a city contractor had completely bulldozed his domicile, with all his possessions in it. Said Mayor Patrick Henry Hays: "It appears the city made a mistake."

Cherokee Blood

A contractor from Tulsa, Oklahoma has obtained $19 million in minority subcontracts on the rapid transit system in Los Angeles—more than any other disadvantaged firm. His name is Jon McGrath, and he is a blue-eyed, fair-skinned Cherokee Indian. Really? Well, one of his grandmothers was 1/16 Indian, and this makes Jon *1/64 Indian.* Which was enough to allow him to join the Cherokee Nation of Oklahoma, which in turn allowed him to claim minority status, which in turn allowed him to gain preferential treatment in the awarding of government contracts—which in turn he used to great personal advantage.

A Good Sign

Ski lift sign in Oregon:

GOING BEYOND
THIS POINT MAY
RESULT IN DEATH
AND/OR LOSS OF
SKIING PRIVILEGES

Christmas Spirit

A retiring worker at the Los Angeles Department of Public Works made an anonymous donation of $1,600 in an envelope marked "For Bureau of Street Lighting Party. Merry Christmas." Simple enough? Not quite. The Public Works director grew concerned over the "propriety" of the gift. He wondered whether it might represent a "conflict of interest." "It was such an exorbitant amount," he said. "We were concerned about what to do with it. It's unheard of." He suggested using only $800 for the party, and donating $800 to a school. But an unsigned memo circulating around the department said that the donor wanted the money to be used exclusively for the party. After the initial excitement over receiving the gift, everyone grew demoralized by the hassling, lost the spirit—*and cancelled the party altogether.*

> *"Power does not corrupt men; fools, however, if they get into a position of power, corrupt power."*
> —George Bernard Shaw

KKK Haberdashery?

The Baltimore city government has set up a special hotline to combat rumors that recurrently sweep the city. Some of the rumors:

* The city was going to build an underwater mall with a restaurant in which you could pick out your dinner through the glass. This rumor was so strong that contractors started calling the city to ask about bidding on the project.
* Citizens could help pay for kidney dialysis by turning in to the city their empty cigarette packs and the pull tabs from soda pop cans.
* A member of the Ku Klux Klan owned a popular line of sweat suits. The rumor had it that the owner said on a television show that blacks will "overpay for everything," so he had decided to put out an expensive line of sweat suits. It turned out that the owner of the company was an unlikely member of the KKK—he was Jewish.

Minority Rights

Baltimore contractor Donald Keister, thirty, wants a chance to bid on some of the contracts the city sets aside for minorities. Why? He considers himself a minority of one who should not be discriminated against—he weights 640 pounds.

Personal Check

A man who runs a nonprofit organization that serves adults with brain injuries complained to California ex-Governor Deukmejian about state budget cuts affecting the poor—the cuts will hurt real people, he protested, "not just a bunch of nameless and faceless numbers." The good governor wrote the man a letter thanking him for his "desire and willingness to pay more taxes . . . If you write a personal check to the state . . . I will make sure that it is immediately deposited."

Picking Tomatos

California's Employment Training Panel awarded a two million dollar contract to the Ventura County Agricultural Association to train 800 new workers. The program called for lectures, instructional videos, and on-the-job training to learn how to pick different crops. How much training? Well, how about *fifty-nine hours* to learn how to pick a tomato.

Milking It

In 1989, the chief of one of Taiwan's milk-producing regions came up with the brilliant idea of digging a 15-by-25-meter swimming pool and filling it with milk. This would increase the demand for milk during the traditionally slow winter season, by exploiting the Chinese belief that milk keeps the skin healthy. To fill the pool would require a day's production from 12,500 cows—one-fifth of the country's total daily milk production. Construction was already underway before those with slightly larger cranial capacity began pointing out the obvious: milk sours in three hours at room temperature; to avoid spoiling, it must be kept refrigerated—and thus too cold for swimming.

Blue Widow

In Oakland, California, a seventy-eight-year-old widow had to sleep in her car for weeks. Why? Because local officials auctioned off her $47,000 home to pay $530 in back taxes they claimed she owed for renting out her house. One little glitch: she had never rented out her house and therefore owed no back taxes.

"In France we threaten the man who rings the alarm bell and leave him in peace who starts the fire." —Chamfort

---

Affirmative Discrimination

One Mr. Arias, a Latino, was accused by his deputy, a black woman, of discriminating against her because of her race. In her complaint, she said, "Mr. Arias is in the business of fostering racial divisiveness and animosity between two groups." This was at least the third discrimination suit filed against Mr. Arias since the mideighties. What is so unusual about this? Mr. Arias is the head of Los Angeles County's Affirmative Action Compliance Office.

Pointy Fingers

One happy Saturday in the Van Nuys area of California, the state highway department (Caltrans) shut down the Ventura freeway for repairs and rerouted traffic on local "surface streets." Unfortunately, the Los Angeles City Department of Transportation had decided to work on those very surface streets on the same day. The ensuing traffic jam clogged streets for miles, virtually shutting down the area. Of course the state insisted that it had notified the city beforehand, and the city insisted that the state had done no such thing.

Generous Refund

In 1990, two Indiana couples were ecstatic when they received their state income tax refunds. One expected $82, but received instead a refund of $8,202,416.48. The other, expecting $300, received $8,202,182.71. Before they could spend the money, however, an embarrassed tax department employee showed up at their doors and sheepishly asked them to return the checks.

Postpartum Care

Federal law requires that California's Medi-Cal applications be processed within forty-five days. In March, 1990, 17,000 applications had been pending for sixty days or longer, including those of pregnant women and newborn infants who had been waiting as long as *fourteen months*—completely eliminating the possibility of prenatal or early postnatal care.

"The art of taxation consists in so plucking the goose as to get the most feathers with the least hissing." —Colbert

---

Molestation Advocate

A veteran Los Angeles County social worker was arrested for allegedly molesting children. He had not been carefully investigated even though he had been writing letters to county supervisors and other officials complaining that the agency was too quick to condemn sexual acts involving children. In the letters, he maintained that a range of sexual conduct—including acts between adults and children—should be researched as inevitable social phenomena rather than investigated as crimes. He wrote, "... We are learning that nonoffenders, probably a very large percentage of our male population, can respond genitally to erotic stimuli related to children and youth." Despite the fact that the man's views were well known before he wrote the letters, he was not removed as supervising social worker until after his arrest.

Water Drop

A woman in Pasadena, California, where there is a perennial water shortage, received a commendation letter from the city because her water consumption had dropped 25 percent since the prior year. The note asked whether she would be willing to have her photograph shown in the local paper, along with the reason for the decrease. This was a little embarrassing: the reason she had used less water during the year was that she had gotten divorced.

Manholes by Another Name

The Sacramento, California, Public Works Department showed its extreme sensitivity to feminist issues by running "The Manhole Terminology Change Contest," to rename the common manhole to something less sexist. The winner? "Maintenance Hole" won out over such exciting entries as "person-access hole."

Guns for Vests

The city of Concord, New Hampshire, made about $2,700 by selling forty guns confiscated from criminals. What did they plan to do with the money? Buy bulletproof vests for the police.

Auto Trial

In 1990 the Bay Area Rapid Transit put an automobile on trial for contributing to the world's ills. Found guilty of polluting the air and clogging the freeways, the car was sentenced to destruction, and demolished with sledgehammers.

Health Hazard

City officials in Bellflower, California, shut down the snow cone stand of two little sisters, six and eight years of age, because they were violating zoning and health codes.

Driving Without a License

Danny Gomez had to appear before a municipal judge in San Pedro, California, on charges of driving without a license, driving without proof of insurance, and running a stop sign. "It wasn't me," said Danny, "I don't drive." Danny is three years old.

"The brain is a wonderful organ; it starts working the moment you get up in the morning and does not stop until you get to the office." —Robert Frost

Safe Flight

A newsman criticized Iowa's Air National Guard, claiming its flying was dangerous. To defuse him, the Guard invited him to go up in one of their fighters during a flight exercise with another fighter. He agreed. Up went the two fighters—and collided.

Numbers Game

City councilman Charles Boyer II felt strongly that the street addresses in Santa Clarita, California, were illogical, so he wanted to change every address in the city. He claimed it was a very simple process. You simply give every street a new set of addresses. But for five years you leave the old numbers on the curb while the new numbers are on the buildings, to ease the transition to the new system. After that you erase the old numbers from the curb. Needless to say, the council decided to stay with the old system.

Expensive Dinner

For twenty years of service, a city employee in Lakeland, Florida, was awarded a plaque and a certificate for a free dinner. Either he felt he had done an awfully good job or he was very hungry: he and a companion ordered three lobster tails, thirty-three jumbo shrimp cocktails, forty-eight steamed oysters, and a variety of steaks and other seafood. The bill? A mere $510. The man's supervisors were not amused. Initially they recommended that he be fired from his $38,771-a-year job; later, they settled for a two-week suspension and a demotion that chopped his pay by over $11,000 a year.

No Littering in Trash Bin

A Santa Monica, California, resident recently tossed some junk mail in a corner refuse barrel. Shortly afterward, he received a letter from the city informing him that he would be fined $25 if he ever again used a public container for his private trash. Said the letter, barrels on city streets are "only for litter produced by the general public."

Poor Lawyers

In 1989, Los Angeles County paid twenty private attorneys five and half million dollars to defend indigent people. This did not include all legal fees for indigents—only the amount paid to the twenty highest-paid attorneys. One of the attorneys made $436,444.

"Fish rot from the head down."   —*Greek proverb*

RELIGION

"If I had been present at creation, I would have given some useful hints." —Alfonso the Wise

Walking on Water

In Bombay, India in 1966, a yogi named Rao announced his intention to walk on water. Prominent members of Bombay society flocked to witness the spectacle, with tickets selling for as high as a hundred dollars apiece. The story was even covered by *Time* magazine.

In flowing robes, the white-bearded yogi stood transcendentally at the edge of a five-foot-deep pond, deep in prayer. He then stepped boldly into history. He sank like a stone.

White Horses

In nineteenth-century Russia, a religious sect named the Skoptzies, considering chastity of more than passing importance, castrated themselves with razors, glass, bone, or hot irons. They even designated levels of merit commensurate with the thoroughness of the task: the "first purification" consisted of removing the testicles and scrotum, while the "second purification," the highest, was awarded for removing the penis also. This earned one the title "Bearer of the Imperial Seal," and made one "worthy of mounting white horses."

Heathen Heaven

In 1880, Henry Ward Beecher, addressing the issue of the Chinese in America: "We have clubbed them, stoned them, burned their houses and murdered some of them; yet they refuse to be converted [to Christianity]. I do not know any way, except to blow them up with nitroglycerin, if we are ever to get them to Heaven."

"If I had been the Virgin Mary, I would have said 'No.' "   —Margaret Smith

---

No Further Prosecutions

During the infamous Spanish Inquisition, Jane Bohorquia, a noblewoman living in Seville, Spain, was arrested for discussing Protestantism with a group of friends. She was pregnant and died while being tortured. Shortly afterward the Holy Office issued a statement: "The Inquisition has discovered that Jane Bohorquia was innocent. Be it therefore known, that no further prosecutions shall be carried on against her."

Holy Cow

Because of religious injunctions, no self-respecting Hindu can kill a calf or cow even if the family is starving and the beast is useless. Hindus do get clever, though:

- Can the farmer help it if a cow kills its own calf by kicking it? It is only incidental that the farmer placed a triangular yoke around the calf's neck which, each time it tried to nurse, jabbed the cow's udder.
- Can the farmer help it if old cows sometimes starve to death? The fact that they have been tethered on very short ropes is beside the point.

Enough's Enough

American Indians of the Northwest used to engage in a practice called the *potlach*. The object of the potlach was to show up your rivals by outperforming them in generosity—giving away more than they did. To shame their competitors, some potlach chiefs not only gave away their wealth, but actually *destroyed* it—food, clothing, money, anything of value—even to the extreme of burning down their own houses.

"The trouble with born-again Christians is that they are an even bigger pain the second time around."
—Herb Caen

Edison Lives—in Japan

After World War II, with religious suppression suddenly lifted, new religions suddenly proliferated in Japan—including some bizarre ones. Among the latter was Denshinkyo, the "electricity religion," which worshipped Thomas Edison.

Portents of Evil

In November 1990, black-cloaked women in Saudi Arabia drove a convoy of fifteen cars through Riyadh, the capital city, to protest lack of women's rights—in particular, the right to obtain a driver's license. Several of the protestors were immediately suspended from their government jobs, and others received threatening phone calls. Islamic activists identified the women as "communists," "secularists," and "American agents." Saudi Arabia's highest religious authority, Sheik Abdulaziz ibn Abdullah ibn Baz, ruled on "the inadmissibility of women driving cars and the necessity of meting out deterrent and appropriate punishment to whoever commits this act again."

Stay Out

Warning in Bangkok's Temple of the Reclining Buddha:

IT IS FORBIDDEN
TO ENTER A WOMAN

EVEN A FOREIGNER
IF DRESSED AS A MAN

Persecution

An Aryan supremacist, Paul Myron Downing of Arieta, California, terrorized his Jewish neighbor by attempting to set fire to the man's house, shooting out the kitchen windows and placing burning crosses on the lawn. Arrested, he was charged with multiple counts of arson, making terrorist threats, shooting at an inhabited dwelling and desecrating a religious symbol. There was only one hitch: Myron's neighbor wasn't Jewish.

"Kill everyone—God will recognize his own."
—*Papal Legate Arnaud*

Chosen Disciple

The late Osel Tendzin (born Thomas Rich) became the first Westerner to head an international sect of Tibetan Buddhism. He followed the Venerable Chogyam Trungpa Rimpoche, a Tibetan monk who had escaped the Chinese occupation, settled in the U.S., and built his church into the largest Buddhist sect in the nation. Before his death in 1987, Trungpa selected Tendzin as his successor. Church officials were stunned in 1988 when they discovered that Tendzin had been infected with the AIDS virus since 1985, yet had continued to have sexual relations with both men and women. The Venerable (and Uncompassionate) Tendzin died in August, 1990, at age forty-seven.

Sign from God

Alejandrina Carmona, fifty-three, went to feed the dog one day in 1990 and saw images in the bathroom window of her house in Montecito Heights, California. One time it was the Virgin Mary, the next it was Jesus on the cross, and then it was Jesus as a child. "It is a gift from God," she said. "He is telling us to convert. . . ." Word got around. Roman Catholic priests showed up and saw that images were formed by light refracted through the textured glass. But such explanations did little to dissuade the faithful. They stood in long lines and climbed forty steps to see the "vision," and many of them placed candles, plastic flowers, and money under the window.

Cryptic Antichrist

Just before Desert Storm, six American soldiers in military intelligence deserted their posts in West Germany and turned up in Gulf Breeze, Florida. Were they involved in some devious Iraqi plot about the upcoming conflict in the Mideast? Not at all. According to people they had confided in, they were merely going to Florida on their own mission to "destroy the Antichrist," who was believed to be in the Pensacola area. And to experience "Rapture" on the beach at Pensacola; they feared that if they didn't make it to the beach in time, they wouldn't go to Heaven.

"Beware of sharks and missionaries' children."
                                        —*Thornton Wilder*

PUBLIC

Dial C for Corrections

When California's Department of Corrections conducted a survey of public attitudes toward the agency, one of every five people made it clear that they thought that the Department of Corrections is a place to have problems solved or to get things fixed. This misapprehension is consistent all over the country—from Maine to California, from Florida to Washington. Departments of Corrections receive hundreds of phone calls asking them to fix problems with social security checks, drivers licenses, and housing code violations. Some citizens become extremely irate when informed of the agency's true mission.

Date Line

The authorized centennial edition of the American Express recounts the many tribulations of a cruise director on a round-the-world cruise. Among them: having to reason with a passenger who demanded a refund because he lost a day when the ship crossed the international date line.

The Weaver's Tale

In Jackson, Mississippi, police pulled over a car that was zig-zagging through traffic and discovered that the driver was blind. A friend in the seat next to him explained that he was directing the blind driver—because he was too drunk to drive himself.

Black Box

A woman chiropractor in Hollywood did a brisk business with a little black box that she claimed could broadcast cures to patients all over the world. She required from the patient only one thing: a drop of blood. This provided the proper wavelength to send the healing radio-therapy waves to precisely the right location and person.

The black box was also capable of remote *diagnosis*. One skeptic tested it by sending in the blood of a male dog. The box had a ready diagnosis: cancer of the womb.

What's in a Name?

Not known for its collective wisdom, the general public often elects politicians based solely on their names. In 1958 a politician unknown in

Massachusetts was elected state treasurer because he had the same name as the candidate for the U.S. Senate—John F. Kennedy. And as recently as 1988 in Massachusetts, an Edward Kennedy and a Robert Kennedy—no relation to the famous family—were respectively elected to the Middlesex County Commission and to the Governor's Council. A more striking example occurred a decade ago in Michigan. Alfred Lawrence Patterson, whose name was similar to that of L. Brooks Patterson, a popular Oakland County prosecutor, was nominated by the Republican party to run for Michigan's Seventeenth Congressional District. There was only one problem: Patterson was a patient in the Northville Regional Psychiatric Hospital. Though unable to get out and vote for himself, he nevertheless defeated two GOP opponents for the nomination.

"Empty vessels make the most sound."
                                                    —English proverb

---

Mummy's the Word

A wine-making society named Summum Bonum has signed up over a hundred people to be mummified after they die. Cost: about $7,500 each. After death, the customer gets steeped for two months in wine, herbs, and chemical preservatives, and is then coated with scented oils and sheathed in linen, fiberglass, polyethylene, and plaster. That's for the base price. For yuppies, other options are available: gold overlays or jeweled body-shaped caskets, at prices of $100,000 and up.

One woman, a radio talk show host, plans to have a microphone in her mummiform casket. A flight nurse wants her casket to have a bronze mask of herself, and the Beatle's "White Album" tucked in beside her. Her husband wants to take the Big Trip with his favorite wrench beside him. Says a costume designer, "If it's true as some Christians say that on Judgment Day Christ will call us up from the grave, then I want to be in the best shape that I can."

The ABCs

At her christening in 1883, Arthur Pepper named his daughter Anna Bertha Cecilia Diana Emily Fanny Gertrude Hypatia Inez Jane Kate Louisa Maud Nora Ophelia Quince Rebecca Sarah Teresa Ulysses Venus Winifred Xenophon Yetty Zeus Pepper—one name for every letter in the alphabet.

Lost in Space

A shopper was lost for three days in a shopping center in Utrecht, the Netherlands. The seventy-year-old woman went Easter shopping in the multistoried complex and—as she told police who finally found her—after she lost her way she was too embarrassed to ask anyone how to get out.

"The public have an insatiable curiosity to know everything—except what is worth knowing."
—Oscar Wilde

Blank Face

In Chula Vista, California, there is a blank billboard. On Thursday, July 18, 1991, between 10,000 and 25,000 people caused traffic jams when they showed up to see on the billboard the face of a young girl who had recently been slain nearby. People had been flocking to the billboard for at least two weeks. One woman claimed to see the *killer's* image, too. "Eventually, her face will fade away, and all we'll see is his face. That's when he'll be caught."

Winning is Everything

In Japan, one meets otherwise intelligent people who claim that logic is something invented in the West to allow westerners to win arguments.

On a Roll

The Japanese have a morning TV show, *Daybreak,* that among other things uses U.S. video clips to make fun of Americans. What type of thing do they like to show?

- The man in Louisiana who turned a room of his house into a shrine honoring a roll of toilet paper he had swiped from Graceland, the Elvis Presley Museum in Memphis.
- The "pierce boom" in California, in which teenagers pierce not only ears for jewelry but also noses, navels, nipples, chins, and fingers.
- A Texas contest in which men reach into a basket full of rattlesnakes to see who can pick up the most without being bitten.

"The people is that part of the state which does not know what it wants."   —G.W.F. Hegel

---

Smart Money

Ever wonder what you would do if you won the lottery? A fellow who won four million dollars in the New York state lottery had it all figured out. When he picked up the first of his annual checks for $148,000, he quit his $38,000-a-year job, threw a big party, and put $10,000 down on each of 10 new Cadillacs. The aftermath? In the next eight months, six of the cars were repossessed, and he had to borrow $200,000 to tide him over to the next check.

Lottomania

When the Florida lottery jackpot reached $100 million in 1990, people went wild, even though the odds of winning were 13,983,816 to 1. One lady flew in from Las Vegas and bought 1,200 tickets. A group of investors called the Miami regional lottery office and offered a check for $13 million in exchange for tickets covering every possible combination.

Winning the lottery does not guarantee happiness, however. A thirty-five-year-old man was pulled from the Miami River while lottery fever rampaged; he had won $10,000 in a scratch-off lottery game. When his body was found, he had $2,505 in his pocket and an empty wine bottle stuck in the front of his pants. Another man, from Orlando, who had won $188,000 in the lottery in 1989, was found dead at a garbage dump after apparently falling asleep in a trash bin, and then getting compacted by a garbage truck. He had less than $10 in his pockets when the body was discovered. A pauper's funeral was planned, after the thirty-nine-year-old man had apparently blown the lottery money on such things as limousine rides and buying rounds of drinks for his friends.

Gimped Blimp

The Goodyear blimp Columbia was cruising along near Carson, California at about a thousand feet when a radio-controlled model airplane started buzzing it, making seven or eight passes. Suddenly the model darted directly into the side of the blimp—which immediately started losing pressure and had to make an emergency landing. Sheriff's deputies arrested the playful owner of the model airplane on suspicion of assault with a deadly weapon.

Vanity of Vanities

In 1990, the state of California recalled personalized license plates bearing slurs against Italians. This, after complaints by Sons of Italy, a fraternal organization that claimed that such plates were deeply offensive to Italian-Americans. There were 333 vanity plates bearing the words *wop* or *dago*—like DAGO ESQ, TOP WOPS, NY DAGO, LIL DAGO, FOXYDAGO, BBOPWOP and 14KWOP. Half of the plate-holders, virtually all Italian-Americans, immediately protested, requesting special hearings to contest the recall. Said a DMV spokesman, "It's amazing that there's such attachment to a license plate."

BRTQLIT

Speaking of designer plates, here's one on the car of a speech therapist: BRTQLIT. Give up? It means "Be articulate." Talk about practicing what you preach.

"The public be damned."   —*W. H. Vanderbilt*

Gas Masks?

Before and after the outbreak of Desert Storm, people flocked to their local surplus stores and bought up all the desert fatigues in sight, creating a business bonanza. This was well-publicized at the time. Less well-known is the sudden interest in *gas masks*—even in places as remote from Iraq as California. One store in Van Nuys sold forty in under two weeks—masks made in Israel, with instructions printed in Hebrew.

Medfly Remedies

Many remember all too well the 1990 assault of the medfly on Los Angeles, and the ensuing controversy over the aerial spraying of the insecticide malathion. Few were aware of the numerous other remedies suggested. One was to control the little beasties by playing the harmonica. That's right—lower F sharp on the harmonica supposedly has the same frequency as the medfly's mating call, so one merely has to lure in and capture the little malefactors by making strange music on the mouth organ. Other ideas:

- Erect loudspeakers in the infested areas and play very loud acid rock music.
- A psychic suggested getting rid of the bugs through psychotronics. In this discipline, a simple device can focus psychic energy from around the planet to eliminate any bug on earth. Stirring up little interest with the au-

thorities, the psychic went ahead on his own, saying it was his "gift to the people of LA."

- An enterprising fellow came up with an electronic bug-zapper that can easily be attached to lamp posts: the light lures them in, the electricity zaps them. But someone pointed out a small drawback: medflys are not attracted by light.

Bill of Rights

A physicist urged a UFO symposium in Pensacola, Florida, to adopt a bill of rights for people from different worlds. He asserted that all humans and extraterrestrials are "children of the creator" with equal rights. The bill would forbid landings without consent of future global authorities and would prohibit alien bases on other planets' satellites.

Of Nylons and Men

When nylon stockings first hit the U.S. market in 1939, women went wild for them. Before they really got rolling, however, along came World War II, nylon was diverted to the making of parachutes, and few stockings were produced. When stockings did hit department stores, they caused near-riots. Nylons were in even shorter supply than young men, most of whom were in the armed services. A survey of women in Tulsa, Oklahoma, asked what they missed most during the war. For every one who said "men," two said "nylons."

"A wise fellow who is also worthless always charms the rabble."   —*Euripides*

Just Average

A few years ago, a fellow wrote an indignant letter to the *London Times*. He had been studying a report from the Ministry of Health, which indicated that half of the children in the United Kingdom were below average weight. He considered this shocking, a disgrace to the nation, and insisted that the government do something about nourishing the nation's children.

Hats off to Honus

By 1990, baseball cards had boomed into a billion dollar industry. A Mickey Mantle 1952 Topps card was going for $7,000. A shop owner in San Luis Obispo was murdered for $10,000 worth of cards. Collectors and those who catered to them had become totally obsessed with these priceless items. Said Lew Lipset, publisher of a monthly newsletter on the subject: "Try to make a living in this hobby and you'll learn about ... deceit, unfair business practices, the lack of truth in advertising, price manipulation, collusion, restraint of trade, patronage, extortion, payoffs and bribes, graft, plagiarism, and, last but not least, hype."

In 1991, a 1910 Honus Wagner card sold for the incredible sum of $451,000.

Kewpie Doll

Between 1912 and 1914, one Rose Cecil O'Neill made a million and a half dollars on her Kewpie Doll. Not only were the dolls themselves a craze, but there were Kewpie books, Kewpie rattles, Kewpie soaps, Kewpie dishes, Kewpie pianos, and Kewpie salt-and-pepper shakers. It even got so bad that women started plucking their eyebrows to imitate the surprised look of the Kewpie.

Abuzz at the Beach

After Miss St. Tropez showed up covered with bandages at the tourist beach in St. Tropez, France, a number of imitators were seen wearing bikinis made of bandages and surgical gauze. Thus commenced the fad of "the medical look." No one realized that the beauty queen had stepped on a beehive.

"If we were to do the Second Coming of Christ in color for a full hour, there would be a considerable number of stations which would decline to carry it on the grounds that a western or a quiz show would be more profitable."   —*Edward R. Murrow*

Earth Day

On April 22, 1990, hundreds of thousands of people met in New York City's Central Park to express their support for Mother Earth and the cause of environmentalism. Unfortunately, it took fifty park sanitation workers all night to clean up the 154.3 tons of litter left by the Earth Day celebrants.

Double Duchess

England's Elizabeth Gunning married the Duke of Hamilton and then the Duke of Argyll. Just think, a *double* duchess! Seven hundred people once flocked to an inn on the way to Yorkshire and stayed up all night just to see her climb into her post chaise the next morning.

Who?

In 1979, eleven people were killed at Riverfront Stadium in Cincinnati by a crowd flocking to see the rock group The Who. Said an onlooker, "I couldn't believe it. They could see the people all piled up and they still tried to climb over them just to get in."

Drawing a Blank

Corporations are continually receiving requests and advice from the public. One request: in the late 1960s, a man called the *Wall Street Journal* to request that they issue a special blank edition for him. He promised to buy a dozen papers a day.

Status Plates

In England, designer license plates are a rage—British drivers consider them a status symbol. For example, one speedster paid $25,000 for a license plate he thought would startle the police when they pulled him over for speeding. The plate? SNAIL. Another example: at a government auction, a London businessman purchased the right to use a vanity plate saying ELV1S. The price? A mere $132,000.

"You don't want to be rude but you have to be careful—there are a lot of strange people out there."
—*Cliff Robertson*

MILITARY

Pearl Harbor

There have long been rumors that the U.S. knew that Japan would attack Pearl Harbor in 1941, but did nothing either because of incompetence or because FDR wanted a catastrophe to propel the country unequivocally into World War II. Is it possible that the U.S. did not anticipate the strike? Starting in 1931, every graduate of the Japanese Naval Academy had to answer the following question as part of his final examination: "How would you carry out a surprise attack on Pearl Harbor?" The question remained on the exam every year until the beginning of the war in the Pacific.

Cool Iraqis

Early in operation Desert Shield, the British troops in the Gulf were sweltering in camouflage uniforms, because four years earlier Britain had sold its entire stock of cool desert uniforms to— guess who?—Iraq.

Mrs. Fields Joins the Army

The U.S. Army in its infinite passion for details has developed a fifteen-page set of specifications for government-issued cookies. For chocolate chip oatmeal cookies, "The cookies shall be well-baked. They shall be browned on the bottom surface and outer edges, but not appreciably browned on the top surface. . . . They shall be wholly intact, free of checks or cracks. . . . The cookies shall be tender and crisp with an appetizing flavor, free of burnt or scorched flavor."

For sandwich cookies, ". . . each cookie shall consist of two round base cakes with a layer of filling between them. . . . The base cakes shall have been uniformly well-baked with a color ranging from not lighter than chip 27885 or darker than chip 13711. . . . The color comparison shall be made under . . . sky daylight with objects held in such a way as to avoid specular refracture. . . ."

"The United States never lost a war or won a conference."
                                            —*Will Rogers*

Harvard Bats

History is full of ideas for "lunatic weapons," such as the World War I brainstorm of mounting anti-Zeppelin guns on frozen clouds. A classic from World War II is "Harvard Bats." In early

1942 the U.S. was looking for a way to attack Japan. Bombing was out of the question because the U.S. had not yet secured any airstrips within striking distance. But then an official had a bright idea: use bats as airplanes. Tie tiny incendiary bombs to their chests and drop them over the Japanese islands. When they landed, the bats would release the bombs by chewing through the strings. The bombs would then explode.

Harvard University was called upon to develop this batty weapon. Dr. Louis Fieser and his staff took nearly two years to develop the bomb and the surgical technique for attaching it to the bat. Testing then began in New Mexico's Carlsbad Caverns—a veritable bat heaven.

Unfortunately, on the very first day of the test program, several bomb-bearing bats escaped. They promptly set fires that demolished not only a two million dollar hangar but also—considerably more important—a general's staff car. The Army cancelled the program.

So the Navy took over. The Navy had a better idea: cool the bats into artificial hibernation. That way, they would sleep during the flight to the target, and therefore not prematurely chew the strings. Scientists from MIT and UCLA went to work on this problem. The first Navy test was conducted in August 1944. The cooled and sleeping bats were dropped from the air in egglike cartons. Unfortunately, most of the bats slept on—with smashing results. The Navy suddenly realized that by that point in the war it would be easier to drop real bombs than these puny bat-borne incendiaries. They too aban-

doned the project that by then had cost the taxpayers millions of dollars.

Dying for Joy

When the Iran-Iraq war of eight years finally
ended on midnight, August 20, 1988, the Iraqis
celebrated by firing rifles, automatic weapons
and artillery into the air for three days. More
people—350—were killed during the celebration
than during the Iranian missile attacks on Bag-
hdad earlier in the year.

The Killer Vending Machine

Between 1983 and 1988, soda vending machines
claimed the lives of five servicemen and injured
thirty-nine others. It seems that many servicemen
tilt these 1000-pound machines either to cop free
soda, or to vent their rage over losing their
money. Injuries included broken fingers, arms,
legs, feet, ankles and pelvises, and punctured
bladders, and fractured skulls. The Army's safety
newsletter *Countermeasures* warned soldiers to
"beware of the 'killer' vending machines."

Prone in the Cabbages

Hitler started World War II by invading Poland
on September 1, 1939. He staged an "incident"
that would give the Nazis an excuse to retaliate
against the Poles. The "incident" was a staged

assault by "Polish" soldiers (Germans in Polish uniforms) on three German facilities: a customs post, a gamekeeper's house, and a radio station. The customs house attackers were to be triggered by a series of three signals. However, they failed to receive the first, so when the second arrived the commander panicked—assuming the third might be imminent—and sneaked his troops into position in a field of standing crops, awaiting nightfall and the attack. Unfortunately, while in the field they were incommunicado; when Hitler postponed the operation, there was no easy way to inform them. Any Poles in nearby fields were undoubtedly flabbergasted when they saw a German army motorcyclist roar into an empty field and hand a message to camouflaged "Polish" soldier lying prone in the cabbages.

"There are three kinds of intelligence—the intelligence of man, the intelligence of the animal, and the intelligence of the military. In that order."
                                        —Gottfried Reinhardt

Sorry, No Mike

The attack on the radio station encountered problems as well. The plan called for a "Polish" announcer (a German masquerading as a Pole) to break into a live broadcast and—with a background of shouts and gunshots—call heatedly for the destruction of Germany. There was only one

small oversight in the planning; when the attacking "Poles" took the radio station, they discovered that it was merely a relay station and
had no broadcasting facilities.

Bombed Out

In 1945, Admiral William Daniel Leahy advised
President Truman on the atom bomb project:
"This is the biggest fool thing we have ever
done. . . . The bomb will never go off, and I speak
as an expert in explosives."

Law of Averages

During World War I, many soldiers took shelter
in bomb craters, on the assumption that it was
extremely improbable that bombs would fall on
the same spot twice. That kind of thinking per-
sisted into World War II. For example, after his
London flat had been grazed by Nazi bombs, one
P.S. Milner-Barry returned to the dwelling and
refused to relocate. He insisted that the law of
averages was in his favor, right up until his flat
got bombed again—with him in it. He should
have known more about the laws of probability:
he was a chess master.

Marshall Field Montgomery

After World War II, British hero Field Marshall
Montgomery visited Hollywood. Sam Goldwyn

gave a dinner for him, inviting many Hollywood celebrities. At the appropriate time, Goldwyn rose from his table, tapped on his wineglass for silence, and cleared his throat. "It gives me great pleasure tonight to welcome to Hollywood a very distinguished soldier. . . ." he said. "Ladies and Gentlemen, I propose a toast to Marshall Field Montgomery." There was a profound, pin-drop silence. Finally, Jack Warner spoke up: "Montgomery Ward, you mean."

The War Plan

Kaiser Wilhelm of Germany was an avid reader. Some say that one cause of World War I was the Kaiser's reading of Admiral Mahan's *The Influence of Sea Power on History*. After reading this book, the Kaiser immediately determined to build a navy that would rival—and eventually exceed—that of Great Britain. The soul of the German fleet was Grand Admiral von Tirpitz. Though he had served for many years as Secretary of the Navy, he was not allowed to know the war plan for his own navy. This was "kept secret by the Naval Staff even from me." On July 30, 1914, when the operational orders were shown to him he discovered the secret: *there was no plan*. The navy, whose existence had been a chief factor in triggering the war, had no active role designed for it when the war came.

"War is much too important a matter to be left to the generals." —Georges Clemenceau

The Russians Are Coming

During World War I, as in all wars, rumors abounded. One that got completely out of hand was a rumor that a seventeen-hour delay in the Liverpool-London railway service was caused by transport of Russian troops who had landed in Scotland and were on their way to reinforce the Western front. After that, anyone whose train was late attributed the delay to "the Russians." Numerous "events" and "sightings" confirmed the rumor:

- Though it was August, the Russians stamped snow off their boots on station platforms—a railway porter was known to have swept up the snow.
- "Strange uniforms" were glimpsed on passing troop trains.
- Ten thousand Russian soldiers were seen marching along the Embankment on their way to Victoria Station.
- The naval battle of Heligoland was explained by those in the know as a diversion to cover the transport of Russian troops to Belgium.
- An Oxford professor knew a colleague who had been summoned to interpret for the Russians.
- A Scottish army officer in Edinburgh saw the Russians with their horses, wearing "long gaily colored coats and big fur caps," and carrying bows and arrows instead of rifles.
- Sir Stuart Coats of Aberdeen wrote to his

brother-in-law in America that 125,000 Cossacks had marched across his estate.
• Dispatches from Amsterdam reported a large force of Russians being rushed to aid in the defense of Paris. In Paris, people hung around the railway stations hoping to see the Cossacks.

Even the Germans heard the rumor. It caused them considerable concern, since they had transferred 70,000 troops to the *Russian* front.

Clever Ming

In 1642, the beleaguered Ming in China were contending with rebel armies camped outside the city of Kaifeng. Desperate, the Ming provincial governor directed one of the stupider moves in military history: he ordered the city's massive dikes broken to destroy the rebel forces. Naturally, the rebels avoided the floodwaters—but the residents of the city were not so lucky. Several hundred thousand drowned. So severe was the flooding that even though the breach in the dam was closed the following year, the mouth of the Yellow River permanently shifted.

Show Time

In September of 1990, the Seaplane Pilots Association held its eleventh annual "Seaplane Fly-in" at Clear Lake in northern California. All of a sudden an *uninvited* World War II seaplane, a clumsy Lockheed P2V, roared in over the crowd and—apparently showboating for the folks on the beach—performed several spectacular aerobatic maneuvers, the last of which was a barrel roll that ended with a fatal, head-first crash into the lake.

"The emperor sent his troops to the field with immense enthusiasm; he will lead them in person—when they return." —Mark Twain

---

Rubber Raft

During World War II, Great Britain established what they called "The Department of Bright Ideas," to review the ideas of ordinary citizens for winning the war. One bright idea: build a rubber raft the size of England that would float in the North Sea and confuse German pilots.

Unconditional Surrender

Less than a month before the end of World War II, Radio San Francisco announced the Potsdam Declaration. The Allies called for an unconditional surrender by Japan, followed by military occupation, demilitarization, and loss of all overseas territories. At the headquarters of Japan's Fifth Naval Aviation Fleet, the call for unconditional surrender brought a burst of derisive laughter from Vice-Admiral Ugaki—obviously a man in close touch with reality. He shouted, "We should be the ones calling for the unconditional surrender of the United Stated, Great Britain, and China!"

Kill Me Mounds

Some redoubtable third world armies are known for hiding tanks behind so-called "kill me" mounds. These are simply mounds of loose soil and rock behind which tanks lie in wait. Unfortunately, the loose earth of such mounds will not stop an anti-tank round and—even worse—the mound itself, usually different in color than the surrounding terrain, advertises the tank's position, crying out, "I'm a tank—kill me!"

Idi's Solution

Former president of Uganda and would-be world statesman Idi Amin made the following sage statement: "I propose getting rid of conventional armaments and replacing them with reasonably priced hydrogen bombs that would be distributed equally throughout the world."

Elevate Them Guns

During the Battle of New Orleans in the War of 1812, General Andrew Jackson rode through the smoke of combat to determine the accuracy of his artillery fire. After scrutinizing the effects, he rode back to his artillerymen and shouted the order, "Boys, elevate them guns a little lower!"

"You can't say civilization don't advance ... for in every war they kill you in a new way."

—*Will Rogers*

SOURCES

Sources are itemized below. Names of the most-referenced newspapers are abbreviated as follows:

AA News = *Ann Arbor [Michigan] News*
LA Daily News = *Los Angeles Daily News*
LA Times = *Los Angeles Times*
WSJ = *Wall Street Journal*

Book sources are listed in the bibliography that follows the itemized list of sources. In the itemized list, the relevant book is indicated (in bold type) by its number in the bibliography. The page number follows the book number. For example:

Blank Masterpiece [Item Title]—6 [Biblio #], 19 [Page #]

ITEMIZED LIST OF SOURCES

CRIME

Fool For a Lawyer—**49**, 165
Beautiful Corterra—*LA Times*, 7/26/90

Drive Safe—*LA Times*, 10/27/90
Wrong Peel—**17**, 133
Relaxed Burglars—*LA Times*, 8/3/90, 11/11/90
Self-Destruct—*LA Times*, 10/5/90
Long Trip—**35**, 150
Needs His Beer—*LA Times*, 10/1/90
Superstitious Burglar—*China Post*, 1988
Fill Her Up—*LA Times*, 6/19/90
Fun For The Whole Family—**35**, 140
Pub(l)ic Exposure—*LA Times*, 9/28/90
Serious Drawing—**35**, 116
Ducking Stool—**35**, 133
Horrible Language—**35**, 84
Magical Powers—*Orange County Register*, 9/20/90
Leaving Things Hanging—**35**, 109
Wrong Store—*AA News*, 7/26/91
Invisible Man—**10**, 188
Bad Directions—*AA News*, 8/1/91
Slow Weapon—*LA Daily News*, 6/8/90

DEATH

Imelda's Man—*Parade Magazine*, 12/30/90
Dearly Departed—*LA Daily News*, 5/27/90
Lord Grimsley's Funeral—**12**, 163
Bruce Lee's Demise—**13**, 181
Quiet Child—**6**, 160
Drilling For . . .—**30**, 94
Tiger Lady—*AA News*, 6/20/91
Oversize Coffin—*ABC Evening News*, 5/19/77
Hearty Appetite—**12**, 160
The Sheik—**42**, 406
Life After Forty?—**30**, 39
Morbidity Tour—*LA Times*, 5/18/90

Cure for Suicide—*China Post,* 1988
Non-Drinkers' Bier—**2,** 231
Serious About A Tan—*Arizona Republic,* 6/8/90

LAW

Double Cross—Unknown
Tennis, Anyone?—*Tennis,* May, 1987
Hammurabi—**35,** 14
Kansas Pi—**12,** 177
Animal Tales—**10,** 28, 128, 133, 140, 156, 162, 195
Bad Rumor—**12,** 133
Objects of Scorn—**10,** 110, 172, 174, 175, 189, 198
Evidence Evidence—*LA Times,* 9/14/90
Go Fly A Kite—**22,** 11
French Pain—**45,** 47
Buggery—Plural For Bug?—**10,** 149, 150
Beyond A Reasonable Doubt?—*Reader's Digest,* 10/90
Getting Carried Away—**10,** 179
Small Ban—*LA Times,* 7/25/90
Lascivious Oldsters—*LA Times,* 7/29/90
Legal Murder—**48,** 243
Dog Teeth—*LA Daily News,* 7/8/90
Don't Bug Me—**10,** 36, 106, 122, 134, 136
Quiet Germans—*AA News,* 9/8/87

ESPIONAGE

Hitler A Soprano?—**12,** 138
Paroxysms of Madness—**50,** 222
The Spy—**16,** 56
Taken to the Cleaners—**9,** 202

LOVE AND SEX

MEDICINE

FEDERAL GOVERNMENTS

Japanese Gaffe—*LA Times,* 9/27/90
Penetration—*LA Times,* 8/23/90
Driving People Crazy—*LA Times,* 7/21/90
Rich Ghosts—*Denver Post,* 5/22/88
Nautical Buttons—*LA Times,* 6/1/90
Sorry, Right Number—*LA Times,* 6/15/90

SUPERSTITION

The Unholy Bath—**10,** 159
Donate Or Die—*WSJ,* 10/10/88
Bulletproof Ointment—*FYEO, FPIR,* 11/4/87
More Immunization—*LA Times,* 12/31/90
Tough Boxers—**51,** 231
Earthquake God—**33,** 96
Witch Hair?—**35,** 59
LBJ's Cargo—**24,** 117
Stripped—*LA Times,* 12/28/90
Stonehenge Lives—In Nebraska—*Carhenge
    Chronicle,* Summer, 1990
Flying for Peace—*LA Times,* 10/9/90
The Great Goddess—*LA Times,* 9/19/90
Keeping A Clear Mind—*LA Times,* 9/14/90
Elves—*WSJ,* 7/13/90
Being Absolutely Clear—*LA Times,* 6/24/90
Weak Cocktails—*LA Times,* 6/24/90
Dirty Money—*LA Times,* 4/28/90
The Goddess That Failed—*LA Times,* 6/7/90
Sacred Paper—**25,** 339
Rules To Live By—**41,** many

ART AND ENTERTAINMENT

Samson—*AA News,* 7/2/91
Blank Masterpiece—**6,** 19
Superstar—**3,** 93

LAWSUITS

Non-Psychic—CBS 60 *Minutes*, 1/10/88
Talk About Debt—*LA Daily News*, 5/27/90
Spirit Of The Law—*AA News*, 7/20/91
Aggressive Pole—*LA Times*, 6/4/90
Condom Conundrum—*LA Times*, 5/18/90
The Bank Robber—*LA Daily News*, 6/8/90
Oops—*LA Daily News*, 6/10/90
Nintendo Wrist—*AA News*, 8/20/91
Gaseous Suit—*Time*, 8/12/91
Stop That Thief—*Time*, 8/12/91
Sensitive Racist—*Time*, 8/12/91
Odoriferous Complaint—*Funny Times*, 9/91
Expensive Tastes—*LA Daily News*, 4/21/90
Annette's Pal?—*LA Times*, 4/27/90
Frivolous Softball—*WSJ*, 6/20/90

PSYCHOLOGY

New Use For Chopsticks—**14**, 66
Hitler's Kindness—**7**, 282
Clean Dirt?—**6**, 42
Hot For Ronnie—*LA Daily News*, 6/28/90
Off To Bed—**6**, 166
Spite House—**21**, 162
Not Hungry—**14**, 48
Keep The Faith, Ivan—*AA News*, 8/13/89
Kamikazee Camels?—*LA Times*, 10/31/90
Short Hammock—**19**, 163
Poor Shoppers—*AA News*, 7/17/91
Status Symbols—**12**, 196
Rats!—**12**, 200
Weird Address—**21**, 106
Image Is Everything—*LA Times*, 11/28/90
Slumming—*WSJ*, 6/15/90
Love in New York—*LA Times*, 5/23/90

Happy Home—**22**, 10
Doggie Video—*Parade Magazine*, 12/30/91
Pet Homes—*LA Times*, 12/26/90
Millie's Outfit—*LA Times*, 9/17/90
Snake Stories—*LA Times*, 9/8/90

POLITICS

A Ford In Your Past—**49**, 116
Reasons Of Ill Health—**49**, 155
Good Deeds—**4**, 159
Democracy Kits—**12**, 141
Fine Duds—**27**, 99
Golden Girl—*The New Republic*, 9/28/87
Ciccolina's Offer—*LA Times*, 8/24/90
The Being Quayles—*LA Times*, 10/31/90
Quayle Mathematics—*LA Times*, 10/24/90
Watergate 1,2, 3 . . . —**18**, 217
Japanese Brawls—**54**, 335
Vodka, Anyone?—**53**, 266
The Tsarina Is Dead—**26**, 536
Bush League—*AA News*, 5/24/91
Slight Oversight—*LA Times*, 9/27/90
Sacred Detector—*LA Times*, 9/18/90
Lots of Doe—*LA Times*, 9/11/90
Catastrophe in Nepal?—*LA Times*, 9/4/90
Jane Fonda's Home—*LA Times*, 8/30/90
Reverse Sting—*LA Times*, 8/29/90
Like Good Christians—**48**, 240
Fort Knox Gold—**48**, 250
The Coolidge Solution—**48**, 223
German Racket—*LA Daily News*, 7/15/90
Rent-A-Crowd—*LA Times*, 7/6/90
Real Cause of Unemployment—**2**, 252
Ambassador X—*AA News*, 1/29/80

MORE CRIME

SCIENCE AND TECHNOLOGY

Hairy Eyeballs—**7**, 296
Fast Martians—**7**, 294
Crazy Legs—**37**, 46
Pinned—**15**, 157
Stop!—**43**, 382
Zambian Astronauts—**7**, 261
The Golden Arm—*LA Times*, 5/5/90

MARRIAGE AND FAMILY

A Pillar of Strength—**31**, 302
All Fired Up—*WSJ*, 7/7/88
Tear Jerker—**6**, 125
One Wife, One Bath—**12**, 255
Bike Wedding—**49**, 45
Children Not Allowed—**29**
Civilized Divorce—**49**, 19
The More The Merrier—**14**, 82
Switch—*CNN News*, 3/8/90
Miscookulation—*LA Times*, 10/18/90
Rose Bowl Baby—*LA Times*, 8/31/90
Attention—*LA Times*, 8/30/90
Childbirth Prohibited—**29**
Compost Wedding—*LA Times*, 7/6/90
Aerial Gift—*ABC TV News*, 7/10/90
Filial Piety—**54**, 169
Empathy Belly—*LA Times*, 5/18/90
Doting Mother—*AA News*, 8/25/91, 8/28/91

STATE AND LOCAL GOVERNMENT

Painful Welcome—*Parade Magazine*, 12/30/90
Getting Together—*AA News*, 6/3/89
Home-Wrecker—*AA News*, 4/2/89
Cherokee Blood—*LA Times*, 12/27/90

RELIGION

Portents of Evil—*LA Times*, 11/15/90
Stay Out—**29**
Persecution—*LA Times*, 9/11/90
Chosen Disciple—*LA Times*, 8/27/90
Sign from God—*LA Times*, 8/17/90
Cryptic Anti-Christ—*LA Times*, 7/20/90

PUBLIC

Dial C for Corrections—*WSJ*, 4/4/88
Date Line—**4**, 93
The Weaver's Tale—**12**, 132
Black Box—**44**, 55
What's In A Name?—*AA News*, 1/26/89
Mummy's The Word—*WSJ*, 11/28/88
The ABC's—**12**, 250
Lost In Space—**49**, 51
Blank Face—*AA News*, 7/20/91
Winning Is Everything—**54**, 236
On A Roll—*LA Times*, 12/31/90
Smart Money—*LA Times*, 9/18/90
Lottomania—*LA Times*, 9/15/90
Gimped Blimp—*LA Times*, 10/1/90
Vanity of Vanities—*LA Times*, 8/21/90
BRTQLIT—*LA Times*, 8/18/90
Gas Masks?—*LA Times*, 8/21/90
Medfly Remedies—*LA Times*, 7/23/90
Bill of Rights—*LA Times*, 7/10/90
Of Nylons and Men—*AA News*, 10/25/89
Just Average—**8**
Hats Off to Honus—*LA Times*, 6/8/90, *WSJ*,
    7/12/90, *NYT*, 4/24/91
Kewpie Doll—**55**, 97
Abuzz at the Beach—**46**, 51
Earth Day—*LA Times*, 4/24/90

MILITARY

BIBLIOGRAPHY

1. Abrahamsen, David. *Confessions of Son of Sam*. Columbia University Press: New York, 1985.

2. Boller, Jr., Paul F. *Presidential Anecdotes*. Penguin Books: New York, 1982.

3. Boller, Jr., Paul and Davis, Ronald. L. *Hollywood Anecdotes*. Ballantine Books: New York, 1987.

4. Boorstin, Daniel J. *The Image*. Atheneum: New York, 1987.

5. Byrne, Robert. *The 637 Best Things Anybody Ever Said*. Ballantine Books: New York, 1982.

6. Cartland, Barbara. *Book of Useless Information*. Bantam Books: New York, 1977.

7. Cerf, Christopher and Navasky, Victor. *The Experts Speak*. Pantheon Books: New York, 1984.

8. Deming, W. Edwards. *Out of the Crisis.* MIT Press: Cambridge, Massachusetts, 1986.

9. Dulles, Allen. *The Craft of Intelligence.* Greenwood Press: Westport, Connecticut, 1977.

10. Evans, E. P. *The Criminal Prosecution and Capital Punishment of Animals.* Faber and Faber: London: 1987.

11. Fadiman, Clifton, Ed. *The Little, Brown Book of Anecdotes.* Little, Brown and Company: Boston, 1985.

12. Felton, Bruce and Fowler, Mark. *Best, Worst and Most Unusual.* Thomas Y. Crowell: New York, 1975.

13. Forbes, Malcolm. *They Went That-A-Way.* Ballantine Books: New York, 1988.

14. Frewin, Leslie. *The World's Worst of Everything.* Leslie Frewin Publishers: London, 1975.

15. Giscard d'Estaing, Valerie-Ann. *The World Almanac Book of Inventions.* World Almanac Publications: New York, 1985.

16. Goffman, Erving. *Strategic Interaction.* Ballantine Books: New York, 1972.

17. Goldberg, Philip. *The Babinski Reflex.* Jeremy P. Tarcher: Los Angeles, 1990.

18. Goldman, William. *Adventures in the Screen Trade*. Warner Books: New York, 1984.

19. Good, Kenneth. *Into the Heart*. Simon & Schuster: New York, 1991.

20. Gordon, Richard. *Great Medical Disasters*. Dorset Press: New York, 1986.

21. Hall, Edward T. *The Hidden Dimension*. Anchor Books: New York, 1969.

22. Hall, Edward T. *Beyond Culture*. Anchor Books: New York, 1981.

23. Hammer, Richard. *Hoodlum Empire*. Playboy Press: Chicago, 1975.

24. Harris, Marvin. *Cows, Pigs, Wars and Witches*. Vintage Books: New York, 1978.

25. Hsu, Francis L. *Rugged Individualism Reconsidered*. The University of Tennessee Press: Knoxville, Tennessee, 1983.

26. Keegan, John. *The Second World War*. Penguin Books: New York, 1989.

27. Klitgaard, Robert. *Tropical Gangsters*. Basic Books: New York, 1990.

28. Laphan, Lewis, Pollan, Michael and Etheridge, Eric. *The Harper's Index Book*. Henry Holt: New York, 1987.

29. Lo Bello, Nino. *English Well Speeched Here.* Price Stern Sloan: Los Angeles, 1986.

30. Long, Kim and Reim, Terry. *Fatal Facts.* Arlington House: New York, 1985.

31. Louis, David. *2201 Fascinating Facts.* Greenwich House: New York, 1983.

32. Lucas, James. *Kommando.* St. Martin's Press: New York, 1985.

33. Lyons, Arthur. *Satan Wants You.* The Mysterious Press: New York, 1988.

34. MacKay, Charles. *Extraordinary Popular Delusions and the Madness of Crowds.* Farrar, Straus and Giroux: New York, 1932.

35. Mannix, Daniel P. *The History of Torture.* Dell: New York, 1983.

36. Marien, Michael, Ed. *Future Survey Annual 1986.* World Future Society: Bethesda, Maryland, 1987.

37. McKenzie, A. E. E. *The Major Achievements of Science.* Simon & Schuster: New York, 1960.

38. Morgan, Chris and Langford, David. *Facts and Fallacies.* John Wiley & Sons: Toronto, 1981.

39. Naito, Hatsuho. *Thunder Gods*. Kodansha International: New York, 1989.

40. Nierenberg, Gerard I. *The Art of Creative Thinking*. Simon & Schuster: New York, 1982.

41. Opie, Iona and Moira, Tatem, Ed. *A Dictionary of Superstitions*. Oxford University Press: Oxford, 1989.

42. Panati, Charles. *Extraordinary Endings of Practically Everything and Everybody*. Harper & Row: New York, 1989.

43. Panati, Charles. *Extraordinary Origins of Everyday Things*. Harper & Row: New York, 1987

44. Phelan, James. *Scandals, Scamps and Scoundrels*. Random House: New York, 1982.

45. Riordan, Hugh Desaix. *Medical Mavericks, Volume I*. Bio-Communications Press: Wichita, Kansas, 1988.

46. Schreiber, Brad. *Weird Wonders and Bizarre Blunders*. Meadowbrook Press: Deephaven, Minnesota, 1989.

47. Shenkman, Richard. *Legends, Lies and Cherished Myths of American History*. William Morrow: New York, 1988.

48. Shenkman, Richard and Reiger, Kurt. *One-Night Stands with American History*. Quill: New York, 1980.

49. Siegel, Jules and Garfinkel, Bernard. *The Journal of the Absurd*. Workman Publishing: New York, 1980.

50. Smith, R. Harris. *OSS*. University of California Press: Berkeley, California, 1972.

51. Spence, Jonathan D. *The Search for Modern China*. W.W. Norton & Company: New York, 1990.

52. Strassberg, Richard E. *The World of K'ung Shang-jen: A Man of Letters in Early Ch'ing China*. Columbia University Press: New York,

53. Tuchman, Barbara W. *The Guns of August*. MacMillan: New York, 1962.

54. Van Wolferen, Karl. *The Enigma of Japanese Power*. Vintage Books: New York, 1990.

55. Vare, Ethlie Ann and Ptacek, Greg. *Mothers of Invention*. William Morrow: New York, 1987.